ON
HOMOSEXUALITY:

LYSIS,
PHAEDRUS,
AND
SYMPOSIUM

ON HOMOSEXUALITY:

LYSIS, PHAEDRUS, *AND* SYMPOSIUM

Translated by
Benjamin Jowett

with Selected Retranslation, Notes, and Introduction by
Eugene O'Connor

PLATO

GREAT BOOKS IN PHILOSOPHY

Prometheus Books
Buffalo, New York

Published 1991 by Prometheus Books
Introduction and selected retranslation copyright © 1990 by
Eugene O'Connor. All rights reserved.

Editorial offices located at 700 East Amherst Street, Buffalo,
New York 14215, and distribution facilities at 59 John Glenn
Drive, Amherst, New York 14228

Library of Congress Catalog Number: 90-63048
ISBN 0-87975-632-2

Printed on acid-free paper in the United States of America

Additional Volumes in Prometheus's Great Books in Philosophy Series

PLATO was born about 427 B.C. into the distinguished Athenian family of Ariston and Perictione. Although interested in politics as a young man, he became disenchanted at the cruel and immoral behavior of Athenian rulers. Some small ray of hope emerged when Athens deposed its dictators and established a democracy; however, when the citizens put the philosopher Socrates on trial and later executed him of impiety, Plato left Athens to travel abroad.

In 387 B.C., Plato finally returned to Athens and created the Academy, an intellectual center for philosophy and science that offered scholarly training in such fields as astronomy, biological sciences, methematics, and political science. From this influential institution emerged Aristotle, Plato's most famous student. Plato dedicated himself to the Academy until his death in about 347 B.C.

During his lifetime Plato wrote a number of important dialogues, which presented and critically analyzed significant philosophical ideas in metaphysics, epistemology, ethics, and social and political philosophy—all of which continue to occupy scholars. His better-known dialogues include: *The Apology, Cratylus, Crito, Euthryphro, Gorgias, The Laws, Meno, Parmenides, Phaedo, Phaedrus, Protagoras, The Republic, The Sophist, The Symposium, Theaetetus,* and *Timaeus.*

Contents

Introduction

Benjamin Jowett's introduction to his translation of Plato's *Symposium* expresses prevalent Victorian, Edwardian, and even later attitudes, particularly in England and America, toward Greek homosexuality. Some excerpts from the introduction will illustrate this "clash of cultures": "The value which he [Plato] attributes to such loves as motives to virtue and philosophy is at variance with modern and Christian notions, but is in accordance with Hellenic sentiment. The opinion of Christendom has not altogether condemned passionate friendships between persons of the same sex, but has certainly not encouraged them, because, though innocent in themselves, in a few temperaments they are liable to degenerate into fearful evil." "We are still more surprised to find that the philosopher is incited to take the first step in his upward progress . . . by the beauty of young men and boys, which was alone capable of inspiring the modern feeling of romance in the Greek mind." Love between males, when it can be compassed at all, may be safely regarded as higher than love of men for women, says Jowett, "because altogether separated from the bodily appetites." But, at its "worst," this passion must be dismissed with such condemnatory adjectives as "shameful," "immoral," and "indecent." How, then, could the Victorian mind reconcile so noble a philosopher with such degrading vice? It would not be easy.

Since Jowett's day much has been done to counter and correct this willful distortion of ancient sexuality. We may now consult, for example, the more sober appraisals of K. J. Dover, *Greek*

11

Homosexuality (1978), and Saara Lilja, *Homosexuality in Republican and Augustan Rome* (1983) to help us redress the oversights of earlier scholarship. Also, perusal of a competently written handbook of classical literature—Lesky* comes to mind—can assist in providing a background for appreciating Plato in his socio-cultural context.

The composition of the *Symposium* owes much to the Greek tradition of "banquet literature," often a collection of informal discussions (in prose or verse) on various topics, including the power of love and the delights of young men and boys. Each of the (male) guests around the table would take his turn contributing to the conversation: in matters of (homo)erotic discourse, they would draw copiously from legend and mythology for exemplars of the noble youth. A famous example of this symposial genre—with which Plato would have been familiar—is the fifth-century collection known under the title *Theognidea* (named for Theognis of Megara), which describes the infatuation the poet feels for the boy Cyrnus, who is praised as being *kalos,* or beautiful. Indeed, a whole body of homoerotic literature grew up around the themes of male beauty and how one ought to woo and win a boy.

The customary social pattern was this: a boy in his teens or, at any rate, a younger man (called an *erōmenos,* or "beloved") was sought out by an older male (called an *erastēs,* or "lover"), who might be already married. Women in classical Athens were kept in virtual seclusion from everyone but their immediate families and their domestic activities were relegated to certain "female" parts of the house. As a consequence, boys and young men—partly by virtue of their being *seen,* whether in the gymnasium, in the streets, or at a sacrifice (as in the *Lysis*)— became natural love-objects.

The adult man acted the role of the aggressive pursuer, who openly courted a younger male. So eager were men's affections, in fact, that boys had to be regularly escorted by tutors to keep from being molested. In no case was a boy to be seen as the aggressor; essentially playing the female role in a society in which

---

*Albin Lesky, *A History of Greek Literature* (New York: T. Y. Crowell, 1966).

well-bred women were largely absent from public life, the boy would, while displaying his beauty and charms, withhold them at first, yielding to the man only after a period of courtship.

Strict rules of conduct bound both parties: adult males could face prosecution for seducing free-born youths, while Athenian boys and young men could be censured for soliciting sexual favors for money. That would make them in effect equal to courtesans, who were hired companions and lacked citizen status.

This *erastēs-erōmenos* (lover-beloved) relationship, although it was sexual and in many ways comparable to typical male-female relations, with the man assuming the dominant role, was meant ideally to be an educative one. The older man instilled in the younger—in essence, "made him pregnant with"—a respect for the requisite masculine virtues of courage and honor. Plato acknowledges the educative value of male-male relations when, for example, he has Alcibiades in the *Symposium* recount how his passion for Socrates (here humorously cast in the role of the beloved boy) has filled him with the pang of philosophy, and when Socrates in the *Phaedrus* describes how the soul of the pederast (literally, "a lover of youths") who is blessed with philosophy will grow wings after a certain cycle of reincarnations. In recent centuries, the word "pederast" has come to be viewed with opprobrium, fit only to describe child molesters. But in ancient Greece the word carried no such negative connotation, and was employed in a very different context.

Still, candor in the expression of love and sexuality would not have shocked Plato's audience as it still does many in our modern, liberated society. Outspokenness in such matters was far more natural to a culture that regularly practiced public fertility festivals, often featuring models of the male and female genitals. Two popular literary genres of the day, comedy and mime (reflecting their rustic origins), indulged in ribald and suggestive language. Aristophanes, the great comic playwright, appears as a prominent speaker in Plato's *Symposium;* in the same dialgoue Socrates is compared by the lovestruck Alcibiades to a randy satyr, a mythological creature that is half-man, half-goat. Socrates' physical appearance and habits—his great, popping eyes, his indifference to comforts, and sudden fits of immobility when overtaken by serious thought—were the stuff of parody. Aris-

tophanes' play *The Clouds* burlesqued Socrates' popularly conceived role as teacher of impressionable youth. Surrounded as
he often was by the brightest young men of Athens, Socrates
jokingly compared himself, in Xenophon's *Symposium,* to a
pander or procurer. These are witty, humorous characterizations
of Socrates to be sure; yet, in the end, Socrates was the best
erastēs of all, the loving adult male teacher who sought to lead
his aristocratic *erōmenoi* (male beloveds) on the road to virtue.
Unfortunately, the popular caricature of Socrates as the old lecher
stayed in the minds of those who would later, during an age
of hysteria and repression that followed a brutal war, charge
him with corrupting the Athenian youth.

Ultimately, to ascertain best what Plato thinks about male-
male love in the context of his philosophy, we must go to Plato's
own words. For the vast majority of readers who are unfamiliar
with Greek this means recourse to a translation. Jowett's late
nineteenth-century versions of the *Lysis, Phaedrus,* and *Symposium,* long a staple for students of Plato, are still excellent
in many respects, and this is our reason for republishing his
translations of these three dialogues which are so central to the
Platonic literature. But we had another purpose in choosing these
particular dialogues, namely, to illustrate the Platonic view of
homosexuality. And here we must acknowledge that Jowett's
Victorian bias fails to include the sexually loaded language that
Plato sometimes employs. While Plato's ideas may be difficult,
or his views unappealing to some, his language is lucid and clear.
I have sought, then, to recapture this lucidity, my modest hope
being that my efforts at clarification will give a better sense of
Plato's words as he wrote them.

In this volume I have emended Jowett in several places.
My own retranslations appear in brackets beside Jowett's text
or in accompanying notes; to take an example, at *Phaedrus*
238d, I emend Jowett's "to be in a divine fury" with [caught
by nymphs]. Where pertinent, I have included some background
information (again appearing in brackets to distinguish my notes
from Jowett's). My retranslations rely on the Greek text of Plato's
dialogues edited by John Burnet (Oxford, 1909, 1910).

Eugene O'Connor

Lysis, or Friendship

PERSONS OF THE DIALOGUE

SOCRATES, *who is the narrator.*   MENEXENUS.
HIPPOTHALES.   LYSIS.
                    CTESIPPUS.

SCENE:—A newly erected Palaestra outside the walls of Athens.   St.III
p.203

I was going from the Academy straight to the Lyceum, intending   a
to take the outer road, which is close under the wall. When
I came to the postern gate of the city, which is by the fountain
of Panops, I fell in with Hippothales, the son of Hieronymus,
and Ctesippus the Paeanian, and a company of young men who
were standing with them. Hippothales, seeing me approach,
asked whence I came and whither I was going.   b

I am going, I replied, from the Academy straight to the
Lyceum.[1]

Then come straight to us, he said, and put in here; you
may as well.

Who are you, I said; and where am I to come?

He showed me an enclosed space and an open door over

[1. A temple dedicated to Arcadian Zeus]

against the wall. And there, he said, is the building at which we all meet: and a goodly company we are.[1]

204   And what is this building, I asked; and what sort of entertainment have you?

The building, he replied, is a newly erected Palaestra; and the entertainment is generally conversation, to which you are welcome.

Thank you, I said; and is there any teacher there?

Yes, he said, your old friend and admirer, Miccus.

Indeed, I replied; he is a very eminent professor.

Are you disposed, he said, to go with me and see them?

b   Yes, I said; but I should like to know first, what is expected of me, and who is the favorite among you.[2]

Some persons have one favorite, Socrates, and some another, he said.

And who is yours? I asked: tell me that, Hippothales.

At this he blushed; and I said to him, O Hippothales, thou son of Hieronymus! do not say that you are, or that you are not, in love; the confession is too late; for I see not only that you are in love, but that you are already far gone in your love.

c   Simple and foolish as I am, the gods have given me the power of understanding these sort of affections.[3]

At this he blushed more and more.

Ctesippus said: I like to see you blushing,[4] Hippothales, and hesitating to tell Socrates the name; when, if he were with you but for a very short time, he would be plagued to death by hearing of nothing else. Indeed, Socrates, he has literally

d   deafened us, and stopped our ears with praises of Lysis; and if he is a little intoxicated, there is every likelihood that we may have our sleep murdered with a cry of Lysis. His performances in prose are bad enough, but nothing at all in comparison with his verse; and when he drenches us with his poems and other

---

[1. "And a goodly company we are." Literally, "we ourselves and others, many and beautiful."]

[2. "The favorite among you." Literally, "who is the beautiful (male) one."]

[3. "These sorts of affections." Rather, "the (male) lover and the (male) beloved."]

[4. "I like to see you blushing." Rather, "it is a refined thing that you are blushing."]

compositions, that is really too bad; and what is even worse, is his manner of singing them to his love; this he does in a voice which is truly appalling, and we cannot help hearing him: and now he has a question put to him by you, and lo! he is blushing.

Who is Lysis? I said: I suppose that he must be young; for the name does not recall any one to me.

Why, he said, his father being a very well-known man, he retains his patronymic, and is not as yet commonly called by his own name; but, although you do not know his name, I am sure that you must know his face, for that is quite enough to distinguish him.

But tell me whose son he is, I said.

He is the eldest son of Democrates, of the deme of Aexonè.

Ah, Hippothales, I said; what a noble and really perfect love you have found! I wish that you would favor me with the exhibition which you have been making to the rest of the company, and then I shall be able to judge whether you know what a lover ought to say about his love, either to the youth himself, or to others.

Nay, Socrates, he said; you surely do not attach any weight to what he is saying.

Do you mean, I said, that you disown the love of the person whom he says that you love?

No; but I deny that I make verses or address compositions to him.

He is not in his right mind, said Ctesippus; he is talking nonsense, and is stark mad.

O Hippothales, I said, if you have ever made any verses or songs in honor of your favorite, I do not want to hear them; but I want to know the purport of them, that I may be able to judge of your mode of approaching your fair one.

Ctesippus will be able to tell you, he said; for if, as he avers, I talk to him of nothing else, he must have a very accurate knowledge and recollection of that.

Yes, indeed, said Ctesippus; I know only too well; and very ridiculous the tale is: for although he is a lover, and very devotedly in love, he has nothing particular to talk about to his beloved which a child might not say. Now is not that ridiculous? He can only speak of the wealth of Democrates, which the whole city celebratres, and grandfather Lysis, and the other ancestors of the youth, and their stud horses, and their victory at the Pythian games, and at the Isthmus, and at Nemea[1] with four horses and single horses; and these he sings and says, and greater twaddle still.[2] For the day before yesterday he made a poem in which he described how Heracles, who was a connection of the family, was entertained by an ancestor of Lysis as his relation; this ancestor

d was himself the son of Zeus and the daughter of the founder of the deme.[3] And these are the sort of old wives' tales which he sings and recites to us, and we are obliged to listen to him.

When I heard this, I said: O ridiculous Hippothales! how can you be making and singing hymns in honor of yourself before you have won?

But my songs and verses, he said, are not in honor of myself, Socrates.

You think not, I said.

But what are they, then? he replied.

e Most assuredly, I said, those songs are all in your own honor; for if you win your beautiful love, your discourses and songs will be a glory to you, and may be truly regarded as hymns of praise composed in honor of you who have conquered and won such a love; but if he slips away from you, the more you have praised him, the more ridiculous you will look at having

206 lost this fairest and best of blessings; and this is the reason why the wiser lover does not praise his beloved until he has won him, because he is afraid of accidents. There is also another danger; the fair, when any one praises or magnifies them, are filled with the spirit of pride and vainglory. Is not that true?

Yes, he said.

And the more vainglorious they are, the more difficult is the capture of them?

[1. The Pythian games were played at Delphi; the Isthmian at Corinth; and the Nemean were held in the sanctuary of Nemean Zeus, in southern Greece.]

[2. "Greater twaddle." Literally, "more out-of-date" (going back to the days of Cronus).]

[3. The demes, or "parishes," were kinship groups. Each deme played a part in local and state administration.]

I believe that.

✳   What should you say of a hunter who frightened away his prey, and made the capture of the animals which he is hunting more difficult?

He would be a bad hunter, that is clear.   206b

Yes; and if, instead of soothing them, he were to infuriate them with words and songs, that would show a great want of wit: don't you agree with me?

Yes.

And now reflect, Hippothales, and see whether you are not guilty of all these errors in writing poetry. For I can hardly suppose that you will affirm a man to be a good poet who injures himself by his poetry.

Assuredly not, he said: I should be a fool if I said that; and this makes me desirous, Socrates, of taking you into my counsels, and I shall be glad of any further advice which you   c may have to offer. Will you tell me by what words or actions I may become endeared to my love?

That is not easy to determine, I said; but if you will bring your love to me, and will let me talk with him, I may perhaps be able to show you how to converse with him, instead of singing and reciting in the fashion of which you are accused.

There will be no difficulty in bringing him, he replied; if you will only go into the house with Ctesippus, and sit down and talk, he will come of himself; for he is fond of listening, Socrates. And as this is the festival of the Hermaea,[1] there   d is no separation of young men and boys, but they are all mixed up together. He will be sure to come: but if he does not come, Ctesippus, with whom he is familiar, and whose relation Menexenus is his great friend, shall call him.

That will be the way, I said. Thereupon I and Ctesippus went towards the Palaestra, and the rest followed.   e

Upon entering we found that the boys had just been sacrificing; and this part of the festival was nearly come to an end. They were all in white array, and games at dice were going on among them. Most of them were in the outer court amusing themselves; but some were in a corner of the Apodyterium[2]

[1. A feast in honor of the god Hermes]
[2. An undressing room]

playing at odd and even with a number of dice, which they took out of little wicker baskets. There was also a circle of lookers on, one of whom was Lysis. He was standing among the other

207 boys and youths, having a crown upon his head, like a fair vision, and not less worthy of praise for his goodness than for his beauty. We left them, and went over to the opposite side of the room, where we found a quiet place, and sat down; and then we began to talk. This attracted Lysis, who was constantly turning round to look at us—he was evidently wanting to come to us. For a time he hesitated and had not the courage to come alone; but first of all, his friend Menexenus came in out of the

b court in the interval of his play, and when he saw Ctesippus and myself, came and sat by us; and then Lysis, seeing him, followed, and sat down with him; and the other boys joined. I should observe that Hippothales, when he saw the crowd, got behind them, where he thought that he would be out of sight of Lysis, lest he should anger him; and there he stood and listened.

I turned to Menexenus, and said: Son of Demophon, which

c of you two youths is the elder?

That is a matter of dispute between us, he said.

And which is the nobler? Is that a matter of dispute too?

Yes, certainly.

And another disputed point us, which is the fairer?

The two boys laughed.

I shan't ask which is the richer, I said; for you two are friends, are you not?

Certainly, they replied.

And friends have all things in common, so that one of you can be no richer than the other, if you say truly that you are friends.

d They assented. I was about to ask which was the juster of the two, and which was the wiser of the two; but at this moment Menexenus was called away by someone who came and said that the gymnastic-master wanted him. As I imagine, he had to offer sacrifice. So he went away, and I asked Lysis some more questions. I dare say, Lysis, I said, that your father and mother love you very much.

That they do, he said.

And they would wish you to be perfectly happy.

Yes.

But do you think that any one is happy who is in the condition   e
of a slave, and who cannot do what he likes?

I should think not indeed, he said.

And if your father and mother love you, and desire that
you should be happy, no one can doubt that they are very ready
to promote your happiness.

Certainly, he replied.

And do they then permit you to do what you like, and
never rebuke you or hinder you from doing what you desire?

Yes, indeed, Socrates; there are a great many things which
they hinder me from doing.

What do you mean? I said. Do they want you to be happy,
and yet hinder you from doing what you like—for example,   208
if you want to mount one of your father's chariots, and take
the reins at a race, they will allow you to do that; they will
prevent you?

Certainly, he said, they will not allow me to do that.

Whom then will they allow?

There is a charioteer, whom my father pays for driving.

And do they trust a hireling more than you? And may he
do what he likes with the horses? And do they pay him for this?

They do.   b

But I dare say that you may take the whip and guide the
mule cart if you like;—they will permit that?

Permit me! no they won't.

Then, I said, may no one use the whip to the mules?

Yes, he said, the muleteer.

And is he a slave or a free man?

A slave, he said.

And do they esteem a slave of more value than you who
are their son? And do they entrust their property to him rather
than to you? and allow him to do what he likes, when you
may not? Answer me now: Are you your own master, or do   c
they not even allow that?

Nay, he said; of course they do not allow that.

Then you have a master?

Yes, my tutor; there he is.

And is he a slave?

To be sure; he is our slave, he replied.

Surely, I said, this is a strange thing, that a free man should be governed by a slave. And what does he do with you?

He takes me to my teachers.

d   You don't mean to say that your teachers also rule over you?

Of course they do.

Then I must say that your father is pleased to inflict many lords and masters on you. But at any rate when you go home to your mother, she will let you have your own way, and will not interfere with your happiness; her wool, or the piece of cloth she is weaving, are at your disposal: I am sure that there is nothing to hinder you from touching her wooden spathe, or her comb, or any other of her spinning implements.

Nay, Socrates, he replied, laughing; not only does she hinder

e   me, but I should be beaten, if I were to touch one of them.

Well, I said, that is amazing. And did you ever behave ill to your father or your mother?

No, indeed, he replied.

But why then are they so terribly anxious to prevent you from being happy and doing as you like?—keeping you all day long in subjection to another, and, in a word, doing nothing which you desire; so that you have no good, as would appear, out of their great possesions, which are under the control of

209   anybody rather than of you, and have no use of your own fair person, which is committed to the care of a shepherd; while you, Lysis, are master of nobody, and can do nothing?

Why, he said, Socrates, the reason is that I am not of age.

I doubt whether that is the real reason, I said; for as far as that goes, I should imagine that your father Democrates, and your mother, do permit you to do many things already, and do not wait until you are of age: for example, if they want anything read or written, you, I presume, would be the first person in the house who is summoned by them.

b   Very true.

And you would be allowed to write or read the letters in any order which you please, or take up the lyre and tune the notes, and play with the fingers, or strike with the plectrum, exactly as you please, and neither father nor mother would interfere with you.

That is true, he said.

Then what can be the reason, Lysis, I said, why they allow you to do the one and not the other?   c

I suppose, he said, that the reason is that I understand the one, and not the other.

Yes, my dear youth, I said, the reason is not any deficiency of years, but a deficiency of knowledge; and whenever your father thinks that you are wiser than he is, he will instantly commit himself and his possessions to you.

That I believe.

Aye, I said; and about your neighbor, too, does not the same rule hold as about your father? If he is satisfied that you know more of housekeeping than he does, will he continue to   d
administer his affairs himself, or will he commit them to you?

I think that he will commit them to me.

And will not the Athenian people, too, entrust their affairs to you when they see that you have wisdom enough for his?

Yes.

Now, I said, let me put a case. Suppose the great king to have an eldest son, who is the Prince of Asia; and you and I go to him and establish to his satisfaction that we are better cooks than his son, will he not entrust to us the prerogative of making   e
soup, and putting in anything that we like while the boiling is going on, rather than to the Prince of Asia, who is his son?

To us, clearly.

And we shall be allowed to throw in salt by handfuls, whereas the son will not be allowed to put in as much as he can take up between his fingers?

Of course.

Or suppose again that the son has bad eyes, will he allow him or will he not allow him, to touch his own eyes if he thinks that he has no knowledge of medicine?   210

He will not allow him.

Whereas, if we are supposed to have a knowledge of medicine, he will allow us to open the eyes wide and sprinkle ashes upon them, because he supposes that we know what is best?

That is true.

And everything in which we appear to him to be wiser than himself or his son he will commit to us?

That is very true, Socrates, he replied.

Then now, my dear youth, I said, you perceive that in things
210b which we know every one will trust us,—Hellenes and barbarians,
men and women,—and we may do as we please, and no one
will like to interfere with us; and we are free, and masters of
others; and these things will be really ours, for we shall turn them
to our good. But in things of which we have no understanding,
no one will trust us to do as seems good to us—they will hinder
 c us as far as they can; and not only strangers, but father and mother,
and the friend, if there be one, who is dearer still, will also hinder
us; and we shall be subject to others; and these things will not
be ours, for we shall turn them to no good. Do you admit that?

He assented.

And shall we ever be friends to others? And will any others
love us, in as far as we are useless to them?

Certainly not.

Neither can your father or mother love you, nor can anybody
love anybody else, in as far as they are useless to them?

No.

 d And therefore, my boy, if you are wise, all men will be
your friends and kindred, for you will be useful and good; but
if you are not wise, neither father, nor mother, nor kindred,
nor any one else, will be your friends. And not having yet attained to wisdom, can you have high thoughts about that of
which you have no thoughts?

How can I? he said.

And you have no wisdom, for you require a teacher?

True.

And you are not conceited, having nothing of which to
be conceited?

Indeed, Socrates, I think not.

 e When I heard him say this, I turned to Hippothales, and
was very nearly making a blunder, for I had a mind to say to
him: That is the way, Hippothales, in which you should talk
to your beloved, humbling and lowering him, and not as you
do, puffing him up and spoiling him. But I saw that he was
in great excitement and confusion at what had been said; and
I remembered that, although he was in the neighborhood, he
did not want to be seen by Lysis, so I thought better and refrained.

In the meantime Menexenus came back and sat down in   211
his place by Lysis; and Lysis, in a childish and affectionate manner, whispered privately in my ear, so that Menexenus should
not hear: Do, Socrates, tell Menexenus what you have been telling
me.

Suppose that you tell him yourself, Lysis, I replied; for I
am sure that you were attending.

That I was, he replied.

Try, then, to remember the words, and be as exact as you
can in repeating them to him, and if you have forgotten anything, ask me again the next time that you see me.   b

I will be sure to do that, Socrates; but go on telling him something new, and let me hear, as long as I am allowed to stay.

I certainly cannot refuse, I said, as you ask me; but then,
as you know, Menexenus is very pugnacious, and therefore you
must come to the rescue if he attempts to upset me.

Yes, indeed, he said; he is very pugnacious, and that is the   c
reason why I want you to argue with him.

That I may make a fool of myself?

No, indeed, he said; but that you may put him down.

That is no easy matter, I replied; for he is a terrible fellow
—a pupil of Ctesippus. And there is Ctesippus: do you see him?

Never mind, Socrates, you shall argue with him.

Well, I suppose I must, I replied.

Hereupon Ctesippus complained that we were talking in
secret, and keeping the feast to ourselves.   d

I shall be happy, I said, to let you have a share. Here is
Lysis, who does not understand something that I was saying,
and wants me to ask Menexenus, who, as he thinks, will be
able to answer.

And why don't you ask him? he said.

Very well, I said, I will ask him; and do you, Menexenus,
answer. But first I must tell you that I am one who from my
childhood upward have set my heart upon a certain thing. All
people have their fancies; some desire horses, and others dogs;   e
and some are fond of gold, and others of honor. Now, I have
no violent desire of any of these things; but I have a passion
for friends; and I would rather have a good friend than the
best cock or quail in the world: I would even go further, and

say than a horse or dog. Yea, by the dog of Egypt, I should greatly prefer a real friend to all the gold of Darius,[1] or even to Darius himself: I am such a lover of friends as that. And

212 when I see you and Lysis, at your early age, so easily possessed of his treasure, and so soon, he of you, and you of him, I am amazed and delighted, seeing that I myself, although I am now advanced in years, am so far from having made a similar acquisition, that I do not even know in what way a friend is acquired. But this is the question which I want to ask you, as you have experience: tell me then, when one loves another, is

b the lover or the beloved the friend; or may either be the friend?

Either, he said, may be the friend.

Do you mean, I said, that if only one of them loves the other, they are mutual friends?

Yes, he said; that is my meaning.

But what if the lover is not loved in return? That is a possible case.

Yes.

Or is, perhaps, even hated? For that is a fancy which lovers sometimes have. Nothing can exceed their love; and yet they

c imagine either that they are not loved in return, or that they are hated. Is not that true?

Yes, he said, quite true.

In that case, the one loves, and the other is loved?

Yes.

Then which is the friend of which? Is the lover the friend of the beloved, whether he be loved in return, or hated; or is the beloved the friend; or is there no friendship at all on either side, unless they both love one another?

There would seem to be none at all.

d Then that is at variance with our former notion [the notion then being that if one of them loved, they were both friends; but now neither is a friend unless they both love].

That appears to be true.

Then no one is a friend to his friend who does not love in return?

I think not.

Then they are not lovers of horses, whom the horses do not love in return; nor lovers of quails, nor of dogs, nor of wine, nor of gymnastic exercises, who have no return of love; no, nor of wisdom, unless wisdom loves them in return. Or perhaps they do love them, but they are not beloved by them; and the poet was wrong who sings:—

e

Happy the man to whom his children are dear, and steeds having single hoofs, and dogs of chase, and the stranger of another land.

I do not think that he was wrong.
Then you think that he is right?
Yes.
Then, Menexenus, the conclusion is, that what is beloved may be dear, whether loving or hating: for example, very young children, too young to love, or even hating their father or mother when they are punished by them, are never dearer to them than at the time when they are hating them.

213

I think that is true, he said.
Then on this view, not the lover, but the beloved, is the friend or dear one; and the hated one, and not the hater, is the enemy?
That is plain.
Then many men are loved by their enemies, and hated by their friends, and are the friends of their enemies, and the enemies of their friends—that follows if the beloved is dear, and not the lover: but this, my dear friend, is an absurdity, or, I should rather say, an impossibility [for the friend to be an enemy and the enemy to be a friend].

b

That, Socrates, I believe to be true.
But then, if not the enemy, the lover will be the friend, of that which is loved?
True.
And the hater will be the enemy of that which is hated?
Certainly.
Yet there is no avoiding the admission in this, as in the preceding instance, that a man may love one who is not his friend, or who may be his enemy. There are cases in which a lover loves, and is not loved, or is perhaps hated; and a man

c

may be the enemy of one who is not his enemy, and is even his friend: for example, when he loves[1] that which does not hate him, or even hates that which loves him.

That appears to be true.

But if the lover is not a friend, nor the beloved a friend, nor both together, what are we to say? Whom are we to call friends to one another? Do any remain?

Indeed, Socrates, I cannot find any.

d   But, O Menexenus! I said, may we not have been altogether wrong in our conclusions?

I am sure that we have been wrong, Socrates, said Lysis. And he blushed at his own words, as if he had not intended to speak, but the words escaped him involuntarily in his eagerness; there was no mistaking his attentive look while he was listening.

I was pleased at the interest which was shown by Lysis, and I wanted to give Menexenus a rest, so I turned to him,

e   and said, I think, Lysis, that what you say is true, and that we, if we had been right, should never have gone so far wrong; let us proceed no further in this direction (for the road seems to be getting troublesome), but take the other in which the poets will be our guide; for they are to us in a manner the fathers

214   and authors of wisdom, and they speak of friends in no light or trivial manner, but God himself, as they say, makes them and draws them to one another; and this they express, if I am not mistaken, in the following words:—

God is ever drawing like towards like, and making them acquainted.

b   I dare say that you have heard those words.

Yes, he said; I have.

And have you not also met with the treatises of philosophers who say that like must love like? They are the people who go talking and writing about nature and the universe.

That is true, he said.

And are they right in saying that?

They may be.

[1. Jowett has mistranslated here. The meaning is, rather, "when he hates that which does not hate him . . ."]

Perhaps, I said, about half right, or probably altogether right, if their meaning were rightly apprehended by us. For the more a bad man has to do with a bad man, and the more nearly he is brought into contact with him, the more he will be likely to hate him, for he injures him, and injurer and injured cannot be friends. Is not that true?

c

Yes, he said.

Then one half of the saying is untrue, if the wicked are like one another?

That is true.

But people really mean, as I suppose, that the good are like one another, and friends to one another; and that the bad, as if often said of them, are never at unity with one another or with themselves, but are passionate and restless: and that which is at variance and enmity with itself is not likely to be in union or harmony with any other thing. Don't you agree to that?

d

Yes, I do.

Then, my friend, those who say that the like is friendly to the like mean to intimate [to speak in riddles], if I do not misapprehend, that the good only is the friend of the good, and of him only; but that the evil never attains to any real friendship, either with good or evil. Do you agree?

He nodded assent.

Then now we know how to answer the question "Who are friends?" for the argument supplies the answer, "That the good are friends."

e

Yes, he said, that is true.

Yes, I replied; and yet I am not quite satisfied with this. Shall I tell you what I suspect? I will. Assuming that like, inasmuch as he is like, is the friend of like, and useful to him— or rather let me try another way of putting the matter: Can like do any good or harm to like which he could not do to himself, or suffer anything from his like which he would not suffer from himself? And if neither can be of any use to the other, how can they be loved by one another? Can they now?

215

They cannot.

And can he who is not loved be a friend?

Certainly not.

But say that the like is not the friend of the like in as far as he is like; still the good may be the friend of the good in as far as he is good.

True.[1]

But then again, will not the good, in as far as he is good, be sufficient for himself? And he who is sufficient wants nothing —that is implied in the word sufficient?

Of course not.

215b   And he who wants nothing will desire [love] nothing?

He will not.

Neither can he love that which he does not desire?[2]

He cannot.

And he who loves not is not a lover or friend?

Clearly not.

What place then is there for friendship, if, when absent, good men have no desire of one another (for when alone they are sufficient for themselves), and when present have no use of one another? How can such persons ever be induced to value one another?

They cannot.

c   And friends they cannot be, unless they value one another?

Very true.

But see now, Lysis, how we are being deceived in all this; are we not entirely wrong?

How is that? he said.

Have I not heard some one say, as I just now recollect, that the like is the greatest enemy of the like, the good of the good?—and in fact he quoted the authority of Hesiod,[3] who

d   says, "That potter quarrels with potter, bard with bard, beggar with beggar"; and of all other things he also says, "That of necessity the most like are most full of envy, strife, and hatred of one another, and the most unlike of friendship. For the poor man is compelled to be the friend of the rich, and the weak

---

[1. The Greek is less assured: "Perhaps."]

[2. Plato is distinguishing different forms of love here: *agapē,* which may be translated as "charity" or "pleasure" (in something); and *philia,* meaning "affection," "friendship," or "fondness" (for a thing). And these are to be further distinguished from *erōs,* which is passionate love.]

[3. Fl. ca. 800 B.C. He is the author of the *Theogony,* or *Birth of the Gods,* and *Works and Days,* concerned with husbandry.]

requires the aid of the strong, and the sick man of the physician; every one who knows not has to love and court him who
knows." And indeed he went on to say in grandiloquent lan-   e
guage, that the idea of friendship existing between similars is
not the truth, but the very reverse of the truth, and that the
most opposed are the most friendly; for that everything desires
not like but unlike: for example, the dry desires the moist, the
cold the hot, the bitter the sweet, the sharp the blunt, the void
the full, the full the void, and so of all other things; for the
opposite is the food of the opposite, whereas like receives nothing from like. And I thought that he was a charming man who   216
said this, and that he spoke well. What do the rest of you say?

I should say, at first hearing, that he is right, said Menexenus.

Then are we to say that the greatest friendship is of opposites?

Exactly.

Yes, Menexenus; but will not that be a monstrous answer?
And will not the all-wise eristics[1] be down upon us in triumph,
and ask, fairly enough, whether love is not the very opposite
of hate? And what answer shall we make to them? Must we   b
not admit that they speak truly?

That we must.

They will ask whether the enemy is the friend of the friend,
or the friend the friend of the enemy?

Neither, he replied.

Well, but is a just man the friend of the unjust, or the
temperate of the intemperate, or the good of the bad?

I do not see how that is possible.

And yet, I said, if friendship goes by contraries, the contraries must be friends.

They must.

Then neither like and like nor unlike and unlike are friends.

I suppose not.

And yet there is a further consideration: may not all these   c
notions of friendship be erroneous? But still may there not be
cases in which that which is neither good nor bad is the friend
of the good?

[1. Eristics: literally, "those (men) given to contradictions."]

How do you mean? he said.

Why really, I said, the truth is that I don't know; but my head is dizzy with thinking of the argument, and therefore I hazard the conjecture, that the beautiful is the friend, as the old proverb says. Beauty is certainly a soft, smooth, slippery thing, and therefore of a nature which easily slips in and permeates our souls. And I further add that the good is the beautiful. You will agree to that?

d

Yes.

This I say from a sort of notion that what is neither good nor evil is the friend of the beautiful and the good, and I will tell you why I am inclined to think this: I assume that there are three principles—the good, the bad, and that which is neither good nor bad. What do you say to that?

I agree.

And neither is the good the friend of the good, nor the evil of the evil, nor the good of the evil;—that the preceding argument will not allow; and therefore the only alternative is— if there be such a thing as friendship or love at all—that what is neither good nor evil must be the friend, either of the good, or of that which is neither good nor evil, for nothing can be the friend of the bad.

e

True.

Nor can like be the friend of like, as we were just now saying.

True.

Then that which is neither good nor evil can have no friend which is neither good nor evil.

That is evident.

Then the good alone is the friend of that only which is neither good nor evil.

217

That may be assumed to be certain.

And does not this seem to put us in the right way? Just remark, that the body which is in health requires neither medical nor any other aid, but is well enough; and the healthy man has no love of the physician, because he is in health.

He has none.

But the sick loves him, because he is sick?

Certainly.

And sickness is an evil, and the art of medicine a good
and useful thing?   217b
Yes.

But the human body, viewed as a body, is neither good
nor evil?
True.

And the body is compelled by reason of disease to court
and make friends of the art of medicine?
Yes.

Then that which is neither good nor evil becomes the friend
of good, by reason of the presence of evil?
That is the inference.

And clearly this must have happened before that which was
neither good nor evil had become altogether corrupted with the
element of evil, for then it would not still desire and love the
good; for, as we were saying, the evil cannot be the friend of   c
the good.
That is impossible.

Further, I must observe that some substances are assimilated when others are present with them; and there are some
which are not assimilated: take, for example, the case of an
ointment or[1] color which is put on another substance.[2]
Very good.

In such a case, is the substance which is anointed the same
as the color or ointment?
What do you mean? he said.   d

This is what I mean, I said: Suppose that I were to cover
your auburn locks with white lead, would they be really white,
or would they only appear to be white?
They would only appear to be white, he replied.

And yet whiteness would be present in them. But that would
not make them at all the more white, notwithstanding the presence of white in them—they would be neither white nor black.
True.

But when old age superinduces in them the same color,

[1. Delete "an ointment or . . ." and "or ointment" further down.]
[2. Add "The thing applied (i.e., the color) is somehow present to that
on which it has been applied."]

then they become assimilated, and are white by the presence
e   of white.

Certainly.

Now I want to know whether in all cases a substance is
assimilated by the presence of another substance; or must the
presence be after a peculiar sort?

The latter, he said.

Then that which is neither good nor evil may be in the
presence of evil, and not be wholly evil, and that has happened
before now?

True.

Then when anything is in the presence of evil, but is not
as yet evil, the presence of good arouses the desire of good in
that thing; but the presence of evil, which makes a thing evil,
takes away the desire and friendship of the good; for that which
218   was once both good and evil has now become evil only, and
the good had no friendship with the evil?

None.

And therefore we say that those who are already wise,
whether gods or men, are no longer lovers of wisdom; nor can
they be lovers of wisdom, who are ignorant to the extent of
being evil, for no evil or ignorant person is a lover of wisdom.
There remain those who have the misfortune to be ignorant,
but are not yet hardened in their ignorance, or void of under-
b   standing, and do not as yet fancy that they know what they
do not know: and therefore those who are the lovers of wisdom are as yet neither good nor bad. But the bad do not love
wisdom any more than the good; for, as we have already seen,
neither unlike is the friend of unlike, nor like of like. You remember that?

Yes, they both said.

And so, Lysis and Menexenus, we have discovered the nature
of friendship: there can be no doubt of that. Friendship is the
love which the neither good nor evil has of the good, when
c   the evil is present, either in the soul, or in the body, or anywhere.

They both agreed and entirely assented, and for a moment
I rejoiced and was satisfied like a huntsman whose prey is within his grasp. But then a suspicion came across me, and I fancied unaccountably that the conclusion was untrue, and I felt

pained, and said, Alas! Lysis and Menexenus, I am afraid that
we have been grasping at a shadow.

Why do you say that? said Menexenus.   d

I am afraid, I said, that the argument about friendship is
false: arguments, like men, are often pretenders.

How is that? he asked.

Well, I said; look at the matter in this way: a friend is
the friend of some one.

Certainly he is.

And has he a motive and object in being a friend, or has
he no motive and object?

He has a motive and object.

And is the object which makes him a friend dear to him,
or neither dear nor hateful to him?

I don't quite follow you, he said.

I do not wonder at that, I said. But perhaps, if I put the   e
matter in another way, you will be able to follow me, and my
own meaning will be clearer to myself. This sick man, as I was
just now saying, is the friend of the physician—is he not?

Yes.

And he is the friend of the physician because of disease,
and for the sake of health?

Yes.

And disease is an evil?

Certainly.

And what of health? I said. Is that good or evil, or neither?

Good, he replied.

And we were saying, I believe, that the body being neither   219
good nor evil, because of disease, that is to say because of evil,
is the friend of medicine, and medicine is a good: and medicine has entered into this friendship for the sake of health, and
health is a good.

True.

And is health a friend, or not a friend?

A friend.

And disease is an enemy?

Yes.

Then that which is neither good nor evil is the friend of   b

1st   thing loved -

the good because of the evil and hateful, and for the sake of the good and the friend?

That is clear.

Then the friend is a friend for the sake of the friend, and because of the enemy?

That is to be inferred.

Then at this point, my boys, let us take heed, and be on our guard against deceptions. I will no more say that the friend is the friend of the friend, and the like of the like, which has been declared by us to be an impossibility; but, in order that this new statement may not delude us, let us attentively examine another point, which is this: medicine, as we were saying, is a friend, or dear to us for the sake of health?

✳ 219c

Yes.

And health is also dear?

Certainly.

And if dear, then dear for the sake of something?

Yes.

And surely this object must also be dear, as is implied in our previous admissions?

Yes.

And that something dear involves something else dear?

Yes.

But then, proceeding in this way, we shall at last come to an end, and arrive at some first principle of friendship or dearness which is not capable of being referred to any other, for d the sake of which, as we maintain, all other things are dear.

Certainly.

My fear is that all those other things, which, as we say, are dear for the sake of that other, are illusions and deceptions only, of which that other is the reality or true principle of friendship. Let me put the matter thus: Suppose the case of a great treasure (this may be a son, who is more precious to his father than all his other treasures); would not the father, who values his son above all things, value other things also for e the sake of his son? I mean, for instance, if he knew that his son had drunk hemlock, and the father thought that wine would save him, he would value the wine?

Certainly.

And also the vessel which contains the wine?

Certainly.

But he does not therefore value the three measures of wine, or the earthern vessel which contains them, equally with [more than] his son? Is not this rather the true state of the case? All this anxiety of his has regard not to the means which are provided for the sake of an object, but to the object for the sake of which they are provided. And although we may often say that gold and silver are highly valued by us, that is not the truth; for the truth is that there is a further object, whatever that may be, which we value most of all, and for the sake of which gold and all our other possessions are acquired by us. Am I not right?

220

Yes, certainly.

And may not the same be said of the friend? That which is only dear to us for the sake of something else is improperly said to be dear, but the truly dear is that in which all these so-called dear friendships terminate.

b

That, he said, appears to be true.

And the truly dear or ultimate principle of friendship is not for the sake of any other or further dear.

True.

Then the notion is at an end that friendship has not any further object. But are we therefore to infer that the good is the friend?

That is my view.

Then is the good loved for the sake of the evil? Let me put the case in this way: Suppose that of the three principles, good, evil, and that which is neither good nor evil, there remained only the good and the neutral, and that evil went far away, and in no way affected soul or body, nor ever at all that class of things which, as we say, are neither good nor evil in themselves;—would the good be of any use, or other than useless to us? For if there were nothing to hurt us any longer, we should have no need of anything that would do us good. Then would be clearly seen that we did but love and desire the good because of the evil, and as the remedy of the evil, which was the disease; but if there had been no disease, there would have been no need of a remedy. Is not this the nature of the good— to be loved because of the evil, by us who are between the two? But there is no use in the good for its own sake.

c

d

I suppose that is true.

Then the final principle of friendship, in which all other friendships which are relative only were supposed by us to

e   terminate, is of another and a different nature from them. For they are called dear because of another dear or friend. But with the true friend or dear, the case is quite the reverse; for that is proved to be dear because of the hated, and if the hated were away, the loved would no longer stay.

That is true, he replied: at least, that is implied in the argument.

But, oh! will you tell me, I said, whether if evil were to perish, we should hunger any more, or thirst any more, or have

221   any similar affection? Or may we suppose that hunger will remain while men and animals remain, but not so as to be hurtful? And the same of thirst and the other affections,—that they will remain, but will not be evil because evil has perished? Or shall I say rather, that to ask what either would be or would not be has no meaning, for who can tell? This only we know, that in our present condition hunger may injure us, and may also benefit us. Is not that true?

Yes.

And in like manner thirst or any similar desire may some-

b   times be a good and sometimes an evil to us, and sometimes neither one nor the other?

To be sure.

But is there any reason why, because evil perishes, that which is not evil should also perish?

None.

Then, even if evil perishes, the desires which are neither good nor evil will remain?

That is evident.

And must not a man love that which he desires and affects? He must.

Then, even if evil perishes, there may still remain some elements of love or friendship?

c   Yes.

But not, if evil is the cause of friendship: for in that case nothing will be the friend of any other thing after the destruction of evil; for the effect cannot remain when the cause is destroyed.

True.

And have we not been saying that the friend loves something for a reason? And the reason was because of the evil which leads the neither good nor evil to love the good?

Very true.

But now our view is changed, and there must be some other cause of friendship?   d

I suppose that there must.

May not the truth be that, as we were saying, desire is the cause of friendship; for that which desires is dear to that which is desired at the time of desire? And may not the other theory have been just a long story about nothing?

That is possibly true.

But surely, I said, he who desires, desires that of which he is in want?

Yes.

And that of which he is in want is dear to him?   e

True.

And he is in want of that of which he is deprived?

Certainly.

Then love, and desire, and friendship would appear to be of the natural or congenial. That, Lysis and Menexenus, is the inference.

They assented.

Then if you are friends, you must have natures which are congenial to one another?

Certainly, they both said.

And I say, my boys, that no one who loves or desires another would ever have loved or desired or affected him,[1] if   222
he had not been in some way congenial to him, either in his soul, or in his character, or in his manners, or in his form.

Yes, yes, said Menexenus. But Lysis was silent.

Then, I said, the conclusion is, that what is of a congenial nature must be loved.

That follows, he said.

Then the true lover, and not the counterfeit, must be loved by this love.

[1. I.e., the (male) beloved.]

b   Lysis and Menexenus gave a faint assent to this; and
Hippothales changed into all manner of colors with delight.

Here, intending to revise the argument, I said: Can we point
out any difference between the congenial and the like? For if
that is possible, then I think, Lysis and Menexenus, there may
be some sense in our argument about friendship. But if the
congenial is only the like, how will you get rid of the other
argument, of the uselessness of like to like in as far as they
are like; for to say that what is useless is dear, would be ab-
c   surd [discordant]? Suppose, then, that we agree to distinguish
between the congenial and the like—in the intoxication of argument, that may perhaps be allowed.

Very true.

And shall we further say that the good is congenial, and
the evil uncongenial to everyone? Or again that the evil is congenial
to the evil, and the good to the good; or that which is neither
good nor evil to that which is neither good nor evil.

They agreed to the latter alternative.

d   Then, my boys, we have again fallen into the old discarded
error; for the unjust will be the friend of the unjust, and the
bad of the bad, as well as the good of the good.

That appears to be true.

But again if we say that the congenial is the same as the
good, in that case the good will only be the friend of the good.

True.

But that too was a position of ours which, as you will
remember, has been already refuted by ourselves.

We remember.

e   Then what is to be done? Or rather is there anything to
be done? I can only, like the wise men who argue in courts,
sum up the arguments. If neither the beloved, nor the lover,
nor the like, nor the unlike, nor the good, nor the congenial,
nor any other of whom we spoke—for there were such a number of them that I can't remember them—if, I say, none of
these are friends, I know not what remains to be said.

223   Here I was going to invite the opinion of some older person, when suddenly we were interrupted by the tutors of Lysis
and Menexenus, who came upon us like an evil apparition with
their brothers, and bade them go home, as it was getting late.

At first, we and the bystanders drove them off; but afterwards, as they would not mind, and only went on shouting in their barbarous dialect, and got angry, and kept calling the boys— they appeared to us to have been drinking rather too much at the Hermaea, which made them difficult to manage—we fairly gave way and broke up the company.

b

I said, however, a few words to the boys at parting: O Menexenus and Lysis, will not the bystanders go away, and say, "Here is a jest; you two boys, and I, an old boy, who would fain be one of you, imagine ourselves to be friends, and we have not as yet been able to discover what is a friend!"

Phaedrus

PERSONS OF THE DIALOGUE

SOCRATES. PHAEDRUS.

SCENE:—Under a plane-tree, by the banks of the Ilissus.

Socrates. My dear Phaedrus, whence come you, and whither are you going?

Phaedrus. I am coming from Lysias the son of Cephalus,[1] and I am going to take a walk outside the wall, for I have been with him ever since dawn, which is a long while, and our common friend Acumenus advises me to walk in the country; he says that this is far more refreshing than walking in the courts.

Soc. There he is right. Lysias then, I suppose, was in the city?

Phaedr. Yes, he was with Epicrates, at the house of Morychus; that house which is near the temple of Olympian Zeus.

Soc. And how did he entertain you? Can I be wrong in supposing that Lysias gave you a feast of discourse?

---

1. [The Lysias referred to in this dialogue is the famed orator (ca. 459–380 B.C.). Known for his simple and precise style, Lysias is said to have composed over 200 speeches, the most renowned in defense of Athenian democracy, restored after the reign of the so-called Thirty Tyrants in 403 B.C.]

Phaedr. You shall hear, if you have leisure to stay and listen.

Soc. And would I not regard the conversation of you and Lysias as "a thing of higher import," as I may say in the words of Pindar, "than any business?"

Phaedr. Will you go on?

c   *Soc.* And will you go on with the narration?

Phaedr. My tale, Socrates, is one of your sort, for the theme which occupied us was love—after a fashion: Lysias imagined a fair youth who was being tempted, but not by a lover; and this was the point: he ingeniously proved that the non-lover should be accepted rather than the lover.

Soc. O that is noble of him. And I wish that he would say a poor man rather than a rich, and an old man rather than a young one; he should meet the case of me, and all of us, and d   then his words would indeed be charming, and of public utility; and I am so eager to hear them that if you walk all the way to Megara, and when you have reached the wall come back, as Herodicus recommends, without going in, I shall not leave you.

Phaedr. What do you mean, Socrates? How can you imag-
228   ine that I, who am quite unpracticed, can remember or do jus-
tice to an elaborate work, which the greatest rhetorician of the day spent a long time in composing. Indeed, I cannot; I would give a great deal if I could.

Soc. I believe that I know Phaedrus about as well as I know myself, and I am very sure that he heard the words of Lysias, not once only, but again and again he made him say b   them, and Lysias was very willing to gratify him; at last, when nothing else would satisfy him, he got hold of the book, and saw what he wanted—this was his morning's occupation—and then when he was tired of sitting, he went out to take a walk, not until, as I believe, he had simply learned by heart the entire discourse, which may not have been very long; and as he was going to take a walk outside the wall in order that he might practice, he saw a certain lover of discourse who had the same complaint as himself;—he saw and rejoiced; now thought he, c   "I shall have a partner in my revels." And he invited him to come with him. But when the lover of discourse asked to hear the tale, he gave himself airs and said, "No I can't," as if he didn't like; although, if the hearer had refused, the end would have been that he would have made him listen whether he would or no. Therefore, Phaedrus, as he will soon speak in any case, begs him to speak at once.

Phaedr. As you don't seem very likely to let me off until I speak in some way, the best thing that I can do is to speak as I best may.

Soc. That is a very true observation of yours.

Phaedr. I will do my best, for believe me, Socrates, I did   d
not learn the very words; O no, but I have a general notion of what he said, and will repeat concisely, and in order, the several arguments by which the case of the non-lover was proved to be superior to that of the lover; let me begin at the beginning.

Soc. Yes, my friend; but you must first of all show what you have got in your left hand under your cloak, for that roll, as I suspect, is the actual discourse. Now, much as I love you, I would not have you suppose that I am going to have your memory exercised upon me, if you have Lysias himself here.   e

Phaedr. Enough; I see that I have no hope of practicing upon you. But if I am to read, where would you please to sit?

Soc. Turn this way; let us go to the Ilissus, and sit down   229
at some quiet spot.

Phaedr. I am fortunate in not having my sandals, and as you never have any, I think that we may go along the brook and cool our feet in the water; this is the easiest way, and at mid-day and in the summer is far from being unpleasant.

Soc. Lead on, and look out for a place in which we can sit down.

Phaedr. Do you see that tallest plane-tree in the distance?

Soc. Yes.

Phaedr. There are shade and gentle breezes, and grass on which we may either sit or lie down.   b

Soc. Move on.

Phaedr. I should like to know, Socrates, whether the place is not somewhere here at which Boreas is said to have carried off Orithyia[1] from the banks of the Ilissus.

Soc. That is the tradition.

[1. Boreas was the north wind; his bride, Orithyia, was the daughter of Erechtheus, a fabulous early king of Atheus.]

Phaedr. And this is the exact spot? The little stream is delightfully clear and bright; I can fancy that there might be maidens playing near.

c   *Soc.* I believe that the spot is not exactly here, but about a quarter of a mile lower down, where you cross to the temple of Agra, and I think that there is some sort of altar of Boreas at the place.

Phaedr. I didn't recollect; but I wish that you would tell me whether you believe this tale.

Soc. The wise are doubtful, and if, like them, I also doubted, there would be nothing very strange in that. I might have a rational explanation that Orithyia was playing with Pharmacia, when a

d   northern gust carried her over the neighboring rocks; and this being the manner of her death, she was said to have been carried away by Boreas. There is a discrepancy, however, about the locality, as according to another version of the story she was taken from the Areopagus, and not from this place. Now I quite acknowledge that the explanations are very nice, but he is not to be envied who has to give them; much labor and ingenuity will be required of him; and when he has once begun, he must go on and rehabilitate centaurs and chimeras dire. Gorgons and winged steeds flow in

e   apace, and numberless other inconceivable and impossible monstrosities and marvels of nature. And if he is skeptical about them, and would fain reduce them all to the rules of probability, this sort of crude philosophy will take up all his time. Now I have certainly not time for this; shall I tell you why? I must first know myself, as the Delphian inscription says; and I should be absurd indeed, if while I am still in ignorance of myself I were to be

230   curious about that which is not my business. And therefore I say farewell to all this; the common opinion is enough for me. For, as I was saying, I want to know not about this, but about myself. Am I indeed a wonder more complicated and swollen with passion than the serpent Typho,[1] or a creature of a gentler and simpler sort, to whom Nature has given a diviner and lowlier destiny? But here let me ask you, friend: Is not this the plane-tree to which you were conducting us?

[1. A monster born from earth that had a hundred heads of dragon shape and a hundred hands and feet.]

Phaedr. Yes, this is the tree.   b

Soc. Yes, indeed, and a fair and shady resting place, full
of summer sounds and scents. There is the lofty and spreading
plane-tree, and the agnus castus high and clustering, in the full-
est bloom and the greatest fragrance; and the stream which
follows beneath the plane-tree is deliciously cold to the feet.
Judging from the ornaments and images, this must be a spot
sacred to Achelous[1] and the Nymphs; moreover, there is a
sweet breeze, and the grasshoppers chirrup; and the greatest   c
charm of all is the grass like a pillow gently sloping to the
head. My dear Phaedrus, you have been an admirable guide.

Phaedr. I always wonder at you, Socrates; for when you
are in the country, you really are like a stranger who is being
led about by a guide. Do you ever cross the border? I rather   d
think that you never venture even outside the gates.[2]

Soc. Very true, my good friend; and I hope that you will
excuse me when you hear the reason, which is, that I am a
lover of knowledge, and the men who dwell in the city are my
teachers, and not the trees, or the country. Though I do, indeed,
believe that you have found a spell with which to draw me
out of the city into the country, as hungry cows are led by
shaking before them a bait of leaves or fruit. For only hold
up the bait of discourse, and you may lead me all around Attica,   e
and over the wide world. And now having arrived, I intend
to lie down, and do you choose any posture in which you can
read best. Begin.

Phaedr. Listen. "You know my views of our common interest, and I do not think that I ought to fail in the subject
of my suit, because I am not your lover: for the kindnesses   231
of lovers are afterwards regretted by them when their passion
ceases, but non-lovers have no time of repentance, because they
are free and not subject to necessity, and they confer their benefits
as far as they are able, in the way which is most conducive
to their own interest. Then again, lovers remember how they
have neglected their interests for the sake of their loves; they   b
consider the benefits which they have conferred on them; and

[1. The longest river in Greece]
[2. I.e., the gates of the city]

when to these they add the troubles which they have endured, they think that they have long ago paid all that is due to them. But the non-lover has no such tormenting recollections; he has never neglected his affairs or quarrelled with his relations; he has no troubles to reckon up, or excuses to allege; for all has gone smoothly with him. What remains, then, but that he should freely do what will gratify the beloved? But you will say that

c the lover is more to be esteemed, because his love is thought to be greater; for he is willing to say and do what is hateful to other men, in order to please his beloved: well, that, if true, is only a proof that he will prefer any future love to his present, and will injure his old love at the pleasure of the new. And how can a man reasonably sacrifice himself to one who is pos-

d sessed with a malady which no experienced person would attempt to cure, for the patient himself admits that he is not in his right mind, and acknowledges that he is wrong in his mind, but is unable, as he says, to control himself. How, if he came to his right mind, could he imagine that the desires were good which he conceived when in his wrong mind? Then again, there are many more non-lovers than lovers; and, therefore, you will have

e a large choice, and are far more likely to find among them a compatible friend. And if you fear common opinion, and would avoid publicity and reproach, the lover, who is always thinking that other men are as emulous of him as he is of them, will

232 be sure to boast of his successes, and make a show of them openly in the pride of his heart;—he wants others to know that his labor has not been lost; but the non-lover is more his own master, and is desirous of solid good, and not of the vainglory of men. Again, the lover may be generally seen and known following the beloved (this is his regular occupation), and when they are observed to exchange two words they are supposed

b to meet about some affair of love, either past or future; but when non-lovers meet, no one asks the reason why, because people know that talking is natural, whether friendship or mere pleasure is the motive. And, again, if you fear the fickleness of friendship, consider that in any other case a quarrel might

c be a mutual calamity; but now, when you have given up what is most precious to you, you will be the great loser, and therefore, you will have reason in being more afraid of the lover, for his

vexations are many, and he is always fancying that everything is against him. And for this reason he debars his beloved from society; he will not have you intimate with the wealthy, lest they should exceed him in wealth, or with men of education, lest they should be his superiors in knowledge; and he is equally afraid of the power of any other good. He would persuade you   d
to have nothing to do with them, in order that he may have you all to himself, and if, out of regard to your own interest, you have more sense than to comply with this desire, a quarrel will ensue. But those who are non-lovers, and whose success in love is the reward of their superiority, will not be jealous of the companions of their beloved, but will rather hate those who refuse to be his companions, thinking that their refusal is a mark of contempt, and that he would be benefited by having companions; more love than hatred may be expected to come of that. Many lovers also have loved the person of a youth   e
before they knew his character, or were acquainted with his domestic relations; so that when their passion had passed away, there is no knowing whether they will continue to be his friends; whereas, in the case of non-lovers who were always friends, the friendship is not lessened by sensual delights; but the recollection   233
of these remains with them, and is an earnest of good things to come. Further, I say that you are likely to be improved by me, whereas the lover will spoil you. For they praise your words and actions in a bad way; partly, they are afraid of offending you, and partly, their judgment is weakened by their passion; for lovers are singular beings when disappointed in love—they   b
deem that painful which is not painful to others, and when successful they cannot help praising that which ought not to give them pleasure; so that the beloved is a far more appropriate object of pity than of envy. But if you listen to me, in the first place, I, in my intercourse with you, shall not regard present enjoyment, but future advantage, being not conquered by love,   c
but conquering myself; nor for small causes taking violent offenses, but even when the cause is great, slowly laying up little wrath—unintentional offenses I shall forgive, and intentional ones I shall try to prevent; and these are the marks of a friendship which will last. But if you think that only a lover can be a firm friend, you ought to consider that, if this were true, we

d   should set small value on sons, or fathers, or mothers; nor should
     we ever have loyal friends, for our love of them arises not from
     passion, but from other associations. Further, if we ought to
     confer favors on those who are the most eager suitors, we ought
     to confer them not on the most virtuous, but on the most needy;
     for they are the persons who will be most relieved, and will
     therefore be the most grateful; and, in general, when you make
e   a feast, invite not your friend, but the beggar and the empty
     soul, for they will love you, and attend you, and come about
     your doors, and will be the best pleased, and the most grateful,
     and will invoke blessings on your head. But, perhaps, you will
     say that you ought not to give to the most importunate, but
     to those who are best able to reward you; nor to the lover only,
234 but to those who are worthy of love; nor to those who will
     enjoy the charm of your youth, but to those who will share
     their goods with you in age; nor to those who, having succeeded,
     will glory in their success to others, but to those who will be
     modest and hold their peace; nor to those who care about you
     for a moment only, but to those who will continue your friends
     for life; nor to those who, when their passion is over, will pick
     a quarrel with you, but rather to those who, when the bloom
b   of youth is over, will show their own virtue. Remember what
     I have said; and consider this also, that friends admonish the
     lover under the idea that his way of life is bad, but no one
     of his kindred ever yet censured the non-lover, or thought that
     he was ill-advised about his own interests.

        "Perhaps you will ask me whether I propose that you should
     indulge every non-lover. To which I reply that not even the
c   lover would advise you to indulge all lovers, for the favor is
     less in the just estimation of the receiver and more difficult to
     hide from the world. Now love ought to be for the advantage
     of both parties and for the injury of neither.

        "I believe that I have said enough; but if there is anything
     more which you desire or which needs to be supplied, ask and
     I will answer."

        Now, Socrates, what do you think? Is not the discourse
     excellent, especially the language?
d   *Soc.* Yes, indeed, admirable; the effect on me was ravish-
     ing. And this I owe to you, Phaedrus, for I observed you while

reading to be in an ecstasy, and thinking that you are more experienced in these matters than I am, I followed your example, and, like you, became inspired with a divine frenzy.

Phaedr. Indeed, you are pleased to be merry.

Soc. Do you mean that I am not in earnest?

Phaedr. Now, don't talk in that way, Socrates, but let me   e
have your real opinion; I adjure you, by the god of friendship, to tell me whether you think that any Hellene could have said more or spoken better on the same subject.

Soc. Well, but are you and I expected to praise the sentiments of the author, or only the clearness, and roundness, and accuracy and tournure of the language? As to the first I willingly submit to your better judgment, for I am unworthy to form an opinion, having only attended to the rhetorical manner; and   235
I was doubting whether Lysias himself would be able to defend that; for I thought, though I speak under correction, that he repeated himself two or three times, either from want of words or from want of pains; and also, he appeared to me wantonly ambitious of showing how well he could say the same thing in two or three ways.

Phaedr. Nonsense, Socrates; that was his exhaustive treat-   b
ment of the subject; for he omitted nothing;—this is the special merit of the speech, and I do not think that anyone could have made a fuller or better.

Soc. I cannot go so far as that with you. Ancient sages, men and women, who have spoken and written of these things, would rise up in judgment against me, if I lightly assented to you.

Phaedr. Who are they, and where did you hear anything   c
better than this?

Soc. I am sure that I must have heard; I don't remember at this moment from whom; perhaps from Sappho the fair, Anacreon the wise;[1] or, possibly, from a prose writer. What makes me say this? Why, because I perceive that my bosom is full, and that I could make another speech as good as that of Lysias, and different. Now I am certain that this is not an invention of my own, for I am conscious that I know nothing, and therefore I can only infer that I have been filled through

---

[1. A Greek lyric poet (ca. 582–485 B.C.)]

d   the ears, like a pitcher from the waters of another, though I
    have actually forgotten in my stupidity who was my informant.

    Phaedr. That is grand. But never mind where you heard
    the discourse or of whom; let that, if you will, be a mystery
    not to be divulged even at my earnest desire. But do as you
    say; promise to make another and better oration of equal length
    on the same subject, with other arguments; and I, like the nine
    archons,[1] will promise to set up a golden image at Delphi,
e   not only of myself, but of you, and as large as life.

    Soc. You are a dear golden simpleton if you suppose me
    to mean that Lysias has altogether missed the mark, and that
    I can make a speech from which all his arguments are to be
    excluded. The worst of authors will say something that is to
    the point. Who, for example, could speak on this thesis of yours
236 without praising the discretion of the non-lover and blaming
    the folly of the lover? These are the commonplaces which must
    come in (for what else is there to be said?) and must be allowed
    and excused; the only merit is in the arrangement of them, for
    there can be none in the invention; but when you leave the
    commonplaces, then there may be some originality.

    Phaedr. I admit that there is reason in that, and I will be
    reasonable too, and will allow you to start with the premiss
b   that the lover is more disordered in his wits than the non-lover;
    and if you go on after that and make a longer and better speech
    than Lysias, and use other arguments, then I say again that
    a statue you shall have of beaten gold, and take your place
    by the colossal offering of the Cypselids[2] at Olympia.

    Soc. Is not the lover serious, because only in fun I lay a
    finger upon his love? And so, Phaedrus, you really imagine that
    I am going to improve upon his ingenuity?

    Phaedr. There I have you as you had me, and you must
c   speak "as you best can," and no mistake. And don't let us have
    the vulgar exchange of "tu quoque"[3] as in a comedy, or compel

---

[1. The archons, or "leaders," were the highest official state officers. In
Athens the nine archons were each elected from one of the ten tribes, and
held judicial and executive offices.]

[2. I.e., the descendants of Cypselus, tyrant of Corinth from ca. 655–625
B.C.]

[3. "You too" (Latin)]

me to say to you as you said to me, "I know Socrates as well as I know myself, and he was wanting to speak, but he gave himself airs." Rather I would have you consider that from this place we stir not until you have unbosomed yourself of the speech; for here are we all alone, and I am stronger, remember, and younger than you; therefore perpend,[1] and do not compel me to use violence.

Soc. But, my sweet Phaedrus, how can I ever compete with Lysias in an extempore speech? He is a master in his art and I am an untaught man.

Phaedr. You see how matters stand; and therefore let there be no more pretenses; for, indeed, I know the word that is irresistible.

Soc. Then don't say it.

Phaedr. Yes, but I will; and my word shall be an oath. "I say, or rather swear"—but what god will be the witness of my oath?—"I swear by this plane-tree, that unless you repeat the discourse here, in the face of the plane-tree, I will never tell you another; never let you have word of another!"

Soc. Villain! I am conquered; the poor lover of discourse has no more to say.

Phaedr. Then why are you still at your tricks?

Soc. I am not going to play tricks now that you have taken the oath, for I cannot allow myself to be starved.

Phaedr. Proceed.

Soc. Shall I tell you what I will do?

Phaedr. What?

Soc. I will veil my face and gallop through the discourse as fast as I can, for if I see you, I shall feel ashamed and not now what to say.

Phaedr. Only go on and you may do as you please.

Soc. Come, O ye Muses, melodious (*ligeīai*), as ye are called, whether you have received this name from the character of your strains, or because the Melians[2] are a musical race, help, O help me in the tale which my good friend desires me to rehearse,

d

e

237

[1. Literally, "understand what I'm telling you"]
[2. Rather, Ligurians (*Ligues* in Greek, similar in sound to *ligeīai* = "melodious"]

for the good of his friend whom he always deemed wise and

b will now deem wiser than ever.

Once upon a time there was a fair boy, or, more properly speaking, a youth; he was very fair and had a great many lovers; and there was one special cunning one, who had persuaded the youth that he did not love him, but he really loved him all the same; and one day as he was playing his addresses to him, he used this very argument—that he ought to accept the non-lover rather than the lover; and his words were as follow:—

c   "All good counsel begins in the same way; a man should know what he is advising about, or his counsel will come to nought. But people imagine that they know about the nature of things, when they don't know about them, and, not agreeing at the beginning, they end, as might be expected, in contradict-ing one another and themselves. Now you and I must not be guilty of the error which we condemn in others; but as our ques-tion is whether the lover or non-lover is to be preferred, let us

d first of all agree in defining the nature and power of love, and then, keeping our eyes upon this and to this appealing let us further inquire whether love brings advantage or disadvantage.

"Everyone sees that love is a desire, and we know also that non-lovers desire the beautiful and good. Now in what way is the lover to be distinguished from the non-lover? Let us note that in every one of us there are two guiding and ruling princi-ples which lead us whither they will; one is the natural desire of pleasure, the other is an acquired opinion which is in search

e of the best; and these two are sometimes in harmony and then again at war, and sometimes the one, sometimes the other conquers. When opinion conquers, and by the help of reason leads us to the best, the conquering principle is called temper-ance; but when desire, which is devoid of reason, rules in us

238 and drags us to pleasure, that power of misrule is called excess. Now excess has many names, and many members, and many forms, and any of these forms when marked gives a name to the bearer of the name, neither honorable nor desirable. The desire of eating, which gets the better of the higher reason and

b the other desires, is called gluttony, and he who is possessed by this is called a glutton; the tyrannical desire of drink, which inclines the possessor of the desire to drink, has a name which is only too obvious; and the same may be said of the whole family of desires and their names, whichever of them happens to be dominant. And now I think that you will perceive the drift of my discourse; but as every spoken word is in a manner plainer than the unspoken, I had better say further that the irrational desire which overcomes the tendency of opinion towards right, and is led away to the enjoyment of beauty, and especially of personal beauty, by the desires which are her kindred—that desire, I say, the conqueror and leader of the rest, and waxing strong from having this very power, is called the power of love."

c

And now, dear Phaedrus, I shall pause for an instant to ask whether you do not think me, as I appear to myself, inspired?

Phaedr. Yes, Socrates, you seem to have a very unusual flow of words.

Soc. Listen to me, then, in silence; for surely the place is holy; so that you must not wonder, if, as I proceed, I appear to be in a divine fury [caught by nymphs] for already I am getting into dithyrambics.[1]

d

Phaedr. That is quite true.

Soc. And that I attribute to you. But hear what follows, and perhaps the fit may be averted; all is in their hands above. And now I will go on talking to my youth. Listen:—

Thus, my friend, we have declared and determined the nature of love. Keeping this in view, let us now inquire what advantage or disadvantage is likely to ensue from the lover or the non-lover to him who accepts their advances.

e

He who is the victim of his passions and the slave of pleasure will of course desire to make his beloved as agreeable to himself as possible. Now to him who is not in his right senses that is agreeable which is not oposed to him, but that which is equal or superior is hateful to him, and therefore the lover will not brook any superiority or equality on the part of his beloved; he is always employed in reducing him to inferiority. And the ignorant is the inferior of the wise, the coward of the brave, the slow of speech of the speaker, the dull of the clever. These

239

[1. Dithyrambics were choral songs sung during the Dionysian festival. Socrates may mean to imply that he is speaking bombastically here.]

are the sort of natural and inherent defects in the mind of the
beloved which enhance the delight of the lover, and there are
acquired defects which he must produce in him, or he will be
deprived of his fleeting joy. And therefore he cannot help being
b   jealous, and will debar him from the advantages of society which
would make a man of him, and especially from that society
which would have given him wisdom. That is to say, he will
be compelled to banish from him divine philosophy, in his
excessive fear lest he should come to be despised in his eyes;
and there is no greater injury which he can inflict on him than
this. Moreover, he will contrive that he shall be wholly ignorant, and in everything dependent on himself; he is to be the
delight of his lover's heart, and a curse to himself. Verily, a
c   lover is a profitable guardian and associate for him in all that
relates to his mind.[1]

Let us next see how his master, whose law of life is pleasure
and not good, will keep and train the body of his servant. Will
he not choose a beloved who is delicate rather than sturdy and
strong? One brought up in shady bowers and not in the bright
sun, not practiced in manly exercises or dried by perspiration,
d   but knowing only a soft and luxurious diet, instead of the hues
of health having only the colors of paint and ornament, and
the rest of a piece?—such a life as anyone can imagine and
which I need not detail at length. But I may sum up all that
I have to say in a word, and pass on. Such a person in war,
or in any of the great exigencies in life, will be the anxiety of
his friends and also of his lover, and certainly not the terror
of his enemies; which nobody can deny.

e   And now let us tell what advantage or disadvantage the
beloved will receive from the guardianship and society of his
lover in the matter of his possessions; that is the next point
to consider. All men will see, and the lover above all men, that
his own first wish is to deprive his beloved of his dearest and
best and most sacred possessions, father, mother, kindred,
240 friends, all of whom he thinks may be hinderers or reprovers
of their sweet converse; he will even cast a jealous eye upon
his gold and silver or other property, because they make him

[1. Said sarcastically, indicating that the lover is anything but.]

a less easy and manageable prey, and hence he is of necessity displeased at the possession of them and rejoices at their loss; and he would like him to be wifeless, childless, homeless, as well; and the longer the better, for the longer he is all this, the longer he will enjoy him.

There are some sort of animals, such as flatterers, which are dangerous and mischievous enough, and yet nature has mingled a temporary pleasure and grace in their composition.   240b You may say that a courtesan is hurtful, and disapprove of such creatures and their practices, and yet for the time they are very pleasant. But the lover is not only mischievous to his love, he is also extremely unpleasant to live with. Equals, as the proverb says, delight in equals; equality of years inclines   c them to the same pleasures, and similarity begets friendship, and yet you may have more than enough even of this, and compulsion is always said to be grievous. Now the lover is not only unlike his beloved, but he forces himself upon him. For he is old[1] and his love is young, and neither day nor night will he leave him if he can help; and necessity and the sting of desire drive   d him on, and allure him with the pleasure which he receives from seeing, hearing, touching, perceiving him. And therefore he is delighted to fasten upon him and to minister to him. But what pleasure or consolation can the beloved be receiving all this time? Must he not feel the extremity of disgust when he looks at an old withered face[2] and the remainder to match, which even in a description is not agreeable, and quite detestable when you   e are forced into daily contact with them; moreover he is jealously watched and guarded against everything and everybody, and has to hear misplaced and exaggerated praises of himself, and censures as inappropriate, which are quite intolerable when the man is sober, and, besides being intolerable, are published all over the world in their shamelessness and wearisomeness when he is drunk.

[1. Rather, "older." The typical *erastēs*, remember, was an adult male, often married, and the *erōmenos* a boy in his teens.]

[2. The Greek is less scathing: "an older face and no longer in its prime." But, considering the average lifespan in antiquity, an adult in his thirties might be considered "old."]

And not only while his love continues is he mischievous and unpleasant, but when his love ceases he becomes a perfidious enemy of him on whom he showered his oaths and prayers and
241   promises, and yet could hardly prevail upon him to tolerate the tedium of his company even from motives of interest. The time of payment arrives, and now he is the servant of another master; instead of love and infatuation, wisdom and temperance are his bosom's lords; the man has changed, but the beloved is not aware of this; he asks for a return and recalls to his recollection former acts and words, for he fancies that he is talking to the same person, and the other, being ashamed and not having the courage to tell him that he has changed, and not knowing how
b   to make good his promises, has now grown virtuous and temperate; he does not want to do as he did or to be as he was before. Therefore he runs away and can but end a defaulter; quick as the spinning of a teetotum[1] he changes pursuit into flight, and the other is compelled to follow him with passion and imprecation, not knowing that he ought never from the first to have accepted a demented lover instead of a sensible non-
c   lover; and that in making such a choice he was yielding to a faithless, morose, envious, disagreeable thing, hurtful to his estate, hurtful to his bodily constitution, and still more hurtful to the cultivation of his mind, which is and ever will be the most honorable possession both of goods and men. Consider this, fair youth, and know that in the friendship of the lover there is no real kindness; he has an appetite and wants to feed upon you.

d   As wolves love lambs so lovers love their loves.

But, as I said before, I am speaking in verse, and therefore I had better make an end; that is enough.
        Phaedr. I thought that you were only half-way and were going to make a similar speech about all the advantages of accepting the non-lover. Why don't you go on?
e   *Soc.* Does not your simplicity observe that I have got out of dithyrambics into epics; and if my censure was in verse, what will my praise be? Don't you see that I am already overtaken

---

1. Lit. an oyster-shell.

[inspired] by the Nymphs to whom you have mischievously exposed me? And therefore I will only add that the non-lover has all the advantages in which the lover is charged with being deficient. And now I will say no more; there has been enough said of both of them. Leaving the tale to its fate, I will cross the river and make the best of my way home, lest a worse thing be inflicted upon me by you.   242

Phaedr. Not yet, Socrates; not until the heat of the day has passed; don't you see that the hour is noon, and the sun is standing over our heads? Let us rather stay and talk over what has been said, and then return in the cool.

Soc. Your love of discourse, Phaedrus, is superhuman, simply marvelous, and I do not believe that there is any one of your contemporaries who in one way or another has either made or been the cause of others making an equal number of speeches. I would except Simmias the Theban,[1] but all the rest are far behind you. And now I do verily believe that you have been the cause of another.   b

Phaedr. That is good news. But what do you mean?

Soc. I mean to say that as I was about to cross the stream the usual sign was given to me; that is the sign which never bids but always forbids me to do what I am going to do; and I thought that I heard a voice saying in my ear that I had been guilty of impiety, and that I must not go away until I had made an atonement. Now I am a diviner, though not a very good one, but I have enough religion for my own needs, as you might say of a bad writer—his writing is good enough for him. And, O my friend, how singularly prophetic is the soul! For at the time I had a sort of misgiving, and, like Ibycus,[2] "I was troubled," and I suspected that I might be receiving honor from men at the expense of sinning against the gods. Now I am aware of the error.   d

Phaedr. What error?

Soc. That was a dreadful speech which you brought with you, and you made me utter one as bad.

[1. One of Socrates' inner circle of friends, who was willing to put up money to secure Socrates' escape from prison and who was with Socrates on the day of his death.]

[2. A sixth-century B.C. lyric poet]

Phaedr. How was that?

Soc. Foolish, I say, and in a degree impious; and what can be more dreadful than this?

Phaedr. Nothing, if the speech was really such as you describe.

Soc. Well, and is not Eros, the son of Aphrodite, a mighty god?

Phaedr. That is the language of mankind about him.

Soc. But that was not the language of Lysias' speech any
e   more than of that other speech uttered through my lips when under the influence of your enchantments, and which I may call yours and not mine. For love, if he be a god or divine, cannot be evil. Yet this was the error of both our speeches. There was also a solemnity about them which was truly charming; they had no truth or honesty in them, and yet they pretended to be something, hoping to succeed in deceiving the manikins
243   of earth and be famous among them. And therefore I must have a purgation. And now I bethink me of an ancient purgation of mythological error which was devised, not by Homer, for he never had the wit to discover why he was blind, but by Stesichorus,[1] who was a philosopher and knew the reason why; and, therefore, when he lost his eyes, for that was the penalty which was inflicted upon him for reviling the lovely Helen, he purged himself. And the purgation was a recantation, which began with the words:—

b   That was a lie of mine when I said that thou never embarkedst on the swift ships, or wentest to the walls of Troy.

And when he had completed his poem, which is called "the recantation," immediately his sight returned to him. Now I will be wiser than either Stesichorus or Homer, in that I am going to make a recantation before I lose mine; and this I will attempt, not as before, veiled and ashamed, but with forehead bold and bare.

Phaedr. There is nothing which I should like better to hear.

[1. Greek lyric poet (ca. 632–553 B.C.). The Helen in question was the wife of Menelaus, king of Sparta. Stesichorus had claimed that not she, but a phantom, went to Troy with Paris.]

Soc. Only think, my good Phaedrus, what an utter want   c
of delicacy was shown in the two discourses; I mean, in my
own and in the one which you recited out of the book. Would
not any one who was himself of a noble and gentle nature,
and who loved or ever had loved a nature like his own, when
he heard us speaking of the petty causes of lovers' jealousies,
and of their exceeding animosities, and the injuries which they
do to their beloved, have imagined that our ideas of love were
taken from some haunt of sailors to which good manners were
unknown[1]—he would certainly never have admitted the justice
of our censure?   d

Phaedr. Certainly not.

Soc. Therefore, because I blush at the thought of this person,
and also because I am afraid of the god Love, I desire to wash
down that gall and vinegar with a wholesome draught; and I
would counsel Lysias not to delay, but to write another discourse,
which shall prove "ceteris paribus" that the lover ought to be
accepted rather than the non-lover.

Phaedr. Be assured that he shall. You shall speak the praises
of the lover, and Lysias shall be made to write them in another
discourse. I will compel him to do this.   e

Soc. You will be true to your nature in that, and therefore
I believe you.

Phaedr. Speak, and fear not.

Soc. But where is the fair youth whom I was addressing,
and who ought to listen, in order that he may not be misled
by one side before he has heard the other?

Phaedr. He is close at hand, and always at your service.

Soc. Know then, fair youth, that the former discourse was
that of a finely scented gentleman, who is all myrrh and fra-   244
grance, named Phaedrus, the son of Vain Man.[2] And this is
the recantation of Stesichorus the pious, who comes from the
town of Desire, and is to the following effect: That was a lie
in which I said that the beloved ought to accept the non-lover

---

[1. "To which good manners were unknown." Rather, "having witnessed
no free-born love (as opposed to one born a slave)."]

[2. In Greek, the patronymic is "son of Pythocles" (i.e., famed for the
Pythian oracle sacred to Apollo).]

and reject the lover, because the one is sane, and the other mad. For that might have been truly said if madness were simply an evil; but there is also a madness which is the special gift of heaven, and the source of the chiefest blessings among men. For prophecy is a madness, and the prophetess at Delphi and the priestesses of Dodona,[1] when out of their senses have conferred great benefits on Hellas, both in public and private life, but when in their senses few or none. And I might also tell you how Sibyl and other persons, who have had the gift of prophecy, have told the future of many an one and guided them aright; but that is obvious, and would be tedious.

There will be more reason in appealing to the ancient inventors of names, who, if they had thought madness a disgrace or dishonor, would never have called prophecy, which is the noblest of arts, by the very same name (*mantikē* [prophetic], *manikē* [mad]) as madness, thus inseparably connecting them; but they must have thought that there was an inspired madness which was no disgrace; for the two words, *mantikē* and *manikē*, are really the same, and the letter t is only a modern and tasteless insertion. And this is confirmed by the name which they gave to the rational investigation of futurity, whether made by the help of birds or other signs; this as supplying from the reasoning faculty insight and information to human thought (*noūs* [mind] and *historia* [inquiry]), they originally termed *oionistikē* [relating to augury], but the word has been lately altered and made sonorous by the modern introduction of the letter omega (*oionistikē* and *oiōnistikē*), and in proportion as (*mantikē* or) prophecy is higher and more perfect than divination both in name and reality, in the same proportion as the ancients testify, is madness superior to a sane mind (*sōphrosynē*), for the one is only of human, but the other of divine origin. Again, where plagues and mightiest woes have bred in a race, owing to some ancient wrath, there madness, lifting up her voice and flying to prayers and rites, has come to the rescue of those who are in need; and he who has part in this gift, and is truly possessed and duly out of his mind, is by the use of purifications and mysteries made whole and delivered from evil, future as well as present,

---

[1. In Epirus, the seat of the most ancient oracle of Zeus]

and has a release from the calamity which afflicts him. There is also a third kind of madness, which is a possession of the Muses; this enters into a delicate and virgin soul, and there inspiring frenzy, awakens lyric and all other numbers; with these adorning the myriad actions of ancient heroes for the instruction of posterity. But he who, not being inspired and having no touch of madness in his soul, comes to the door and thinks that he will get into the temple by the help of art—he, I say, and his poetry are not admitted; the sane man is nowhere at all when he enters into rivalry with the madman.

I might tell of many other noble deeds which have sprung from inspired madness. And therefore, let no one frighten or flutter us by saying that temperate love is preferable to mad love, but let him further show, if he would carry off the palm, that love is not sent by the gods for any good to lover or beloved. And we, on our part, will prove in answer to him that the madness of love is the greatest of heaven's blessings, and the proof shall be one which the wise will receive, and the witling disbelieve. And, first of all, let us inquire what is truth about the affections and actions of the soul, divine as well as human. And thus we begin our proof:

The soul is immortal, for that is immortal which is ever in motion; but that which moves and is moved by another, in ceasing to move ceases to live. Therefore, only that which is self-moving, never failing of self, never ceases to move, and is the fountain and beginning of motion to all that moves besides. Now, the beginning is unbegotten, for that which is begotten has a beginning; but the beginning has no beginning, for if a beginning were begotten of something, that would have no beginning. But that which is unbegotten must also be indestructible; for if beginning were destroyed, there could be no beginning out of anything, nor anything out of a beginning; and all things must have a beginning. And therefore the self-moving is the beginning of motion; and this can neither be destroyed nor begotten, for in that case the whole heavens and all generation would collapse and stand still, and never again have motion or birth. But if the self-moving is immortal, he who affirms that self-motion is the very idea and essence of the soul will not be put to confusion. For the body which is moved from

245

b

c

d

e

without is soulless; but that which is moved from within has a soul, and this is involved in the nature of the soul. But if the soul be truly affirmed to be the self-moving, then must she also be without beginning, and immortal. Enough of the soul's immortality.

246

Her form is a theme of divine and large discourse; human language may, however, speak of this briefly, and in a figure. Let our figure be of a composite nature—a pair of winged horses and a charioteer. Now the winged horses and the charioteer of the gods are all of them noble, and of noble breed, while ours are mixed; and we have a charioteer who drives them in a pair, and one of them is noble and of noble origin, and the other is ignoble and of ignoble origin; and, as might be expected, there is a great deal of trouble in managing them. I will endeavor to explain to you in what way the mortal differs from the immortal creature. The soul or animate being has the care of the inanimate, and traverses the whole heaven in diverse forms appearing;—when perfect and fully winged she soars upward, and is the ruler of the universe; while the imperfect soul loses her feathers, and drooping in her flight at last settles on the solid ground—there, finding a home, she receives an earthly frame which appears to be self-moved, but is really moved by her power; and this composition of soul and body is called a living and mortal creature. For no such union can be reasonably believed, or at all proved to be other than mortal; although fancy may imagine a god whom, not having seen nor surely known, we invent—such an one, an immortal creature having a body, and having also a soul which have been united in all time. Let that, however, be as God wills, and be spoken of acceptably to him. But the reason why the soul loses her feathers should be explained, and is as follows:

The wing is intended to soar aloft and carry that which gravitates downwards into the upper region, which is the dwelling of the gods; and this is that element of the body which is most akin to the divine. Now the divine is beauty, wisdom, goodness, and the like; and by these the wing of the soul is nourished, and grows apace; but when fed upon evil and foulness, and the like, wastes and falls away. Zeus, the mighty lord holding the reins of a winged chariot, leads the way in heaven,

b

c

d

e

ordering all and caring for all; and there follows him the heavenly array of gods and demi-gods, divided into eleven bands; 247 for only Hestia[1] is left at home in the house of heaven; but the rest of the twelve greater deities march in their appointed order. And they see in the interior of heaven many blessed sights; and there are ways to and fro, along which the happy gods are passing, each one fulfilling his own work; and anyone may follow who pleases, for jealousy has no place in the heavenly choir. This is within the heaven. But when they go to feast and festival, then they move right up the steep ascent, and mount the top of the dome of heaven. Now the chariots of the gods, b self-balanced, upward glide in obedience to the rein; but the others have a difficulty, for the steed who has evil in him, if he has not been properly trained by the charioteer, gravitates and inclines and sinks towards the earth:—and this is the hour of agony and extremest conflict of the soul. For the immortal souls, when they are at the end of their course, go out and stand upon the back of heaven, and the revolution of the spheres c carries them round, and they behold the world beyond. Now of the heaven which is above the heavens, no earthly poet has sung or ever will sing in a worthy manner. But I must tell, for I am bound to speak truly when speaking of the truth. The colorless and formless and intangible essence is visible to the mind, which is the only lord of the soul. Circling around this in the region above the heavens is the place of true knowledge. And as the divine intelligence, and that of every other soul which d is rightly nourished, is fed upon mind and pure knowledge, such an intelligent soul is glad at once more beholding being; and feeding on the sight of truth is replenished, until the revolution of the worlds brings her round again to the same place. During the revolution she beholds justice, temperance, and knowledge absolute, not in the form of generation or of relation, which men call existence, but knowledge absolute in existence absolute; e and beholding other existences in like manner, and feeding upon them, she passes down into the interior of the heavens and returns home, and there the charioteer putting up his horses at the stall, gives them ambrosia to eat and nectar to drink.

[1. The goddess of the hearth]

248   This is the life of the gods; but of other souls, that which
follows God best and is likest to him lifts the head of the charioteer into the outer world, and is carried round in the revolution, troubled indeed by the steeds, and beholding true being,
but hardly; another rises and falls, and sees, and again fails to
see by reason of the unruliness of the steeds. The rest of the
souls are also longing after the upper world and they all follow, but not being strong enough they sink into the gulf, as
b   they are carried round, plunging, treading on one another, striv-
ing to be first; and there is confusion and extremity of effort,[1]
and many of them are lamed or have their wings broken through
the ill-driving of the charioteers; and all of them after a fruit-
less toil go away without being initiated into the mysteries of
being, and are nursed with the food of opinion. The reason
of their great desire to behold the plain truth is that the food
c   which is suited to the highest part of the soul comes out of
that meadow; and the wing on which the soul soars is nourished with this. And there is a law of the goddess Retribution,
that the soul which attains any vision of truth in company with
the god is preserved from harm until the next period, and he
who always attains is always unharmed. But when she is unable
to follow, and fails to behold the vision of truth, and through
some ill-hap sinks beneath the double load of forgetfulness and
vice, and her feathers fall from her and she drops to earth, then
d   the law ordains that this soul shall in the first generation pass,
not into that of any other animal, but only of man; and the
soul which has seen most of truth shall come to the birth as
a philosopher, or artist, musician, or lover; that which has seen
truth in the second degree shall be a righteous king or warrior
or lord; the soul which is of the third class shall be a politician,
or economist, or trader; the fourth shall be a lover of gymnastic
e   toils, or a physician; the fifth a prophet or hierophant; to the
sixth a poet or imitator will be appropriate; to the seventh the
life of an artisan or husbandman; to the eighth that of a sophist
or demagogue; to the ninth that of a tyrant;—all these are states
of probation, in which he who lives righteously improves, and
he who lives unrighteously deteriorates his lot.

[1. Plato makes clear that it is a sweaty effort (*hidrōs*).]

Ten thousand years must elapse before the soul can return to the place from whence she came, for she cannot grow her wings in less; only the soul of a philosopher, guileless and true, or the soul of a lover,[1] who is not without philosophy, may acquire wings in the third recurring period of a thousand years; and if they choose this life three times in succession, then they have their wings given them, and go away at the end of three thousand years. But the others receive judgment when they have completed their first life, and after the judgment they go, some of them to the houses of correction which are under the earth, and are punished; others to some place in heaven whither they are lightly borne by justice, and there they live in a manner worthy of the life which they led here when in the form of men. And at the end of the first thousand years the good souls and also the evil souls both come to cast lots and choose their second life, and they may take any that they like. And then the soul of the man may pass into the life of a beast, or from the beast again into the man. But the soul of him who has never seen the truth will not pass into the human form, for man ought to have intelligence, as they say, "secundum speciem,"[2] proceeding from many particulars of sense to one conception of reason; and this is the recollection of those things which our soul once saw when in company with God—when looking down from above on that which we now call being and upwards towards the true being. And therefore the mind of the philosopher alone has wings; and this is just, for he is always, according to the measure of his abilities, clinging in recollection to those things in which God abides, and in beholding which He is what he is. And he who employs aright these memories is ever being initiated in perfect mysteries and alone becomes truly perfect. But, as he forgets earthly interests and is rapt in the divine, the vulgar deem him mad, and rebuke him; they do not see that he is inspired.

Thus far I have been speaking of the fourth and last kind of madness, which is imputed to him who, when he sees the beauty of earth, is transported with the recollection of the true

249

b

c

d

[1. Specifically, a pederast, or lover of youths]
[2. "According to his nature" (Latin)]

beauty; he would like to fly away, but he cannot; he is like a
bird fluttering and looking upward and careless of the world
e   below; and he is therefore esteemed mad. And I have shown
that this is of all inspirations the noblest and best, and comes
of the best, and that he who has part or lot in this madness
is called a lover of the beautiful. For as has been already said,
every soul of man has in the way of nature beheld true being;
250 this was the condition of her passing into the form of man. But
all men do not easily recall the things of the other world; they
may have seen them for a short time only, or they may have
been unfortunate when they fell to earth, and may have lost the
memory of the holy things which they saw there through some
evil and corrupting association. Few there are who retain the
remembrance of them sufficiently; and they, when they behold
any image of that other world, are rapt in amazement; but they
are ignorant of what this means, because they have no clear
b   perceptions. For there is no light in the earthly copies of justice or temperance or any of the higher qualities which are precious to souls: they are seen but through a glass dimly; and there
are few who, going to the images, behold in them the realities,
and they only with difficulty. They might have seen beauty shining in brightness, when, with the happy band following in the
train of Zeus, as we philosophers did, or with other gods as
others did, they saw a vision and were initated into most blessed
c   mysteries, which we celebrated in our state of innocence; and
having no feeling of evils as yet to come; beholding apparitions
innocent and simple and calm and happy as in a mystery; shining in pure light, pure ourselves and not yet enshrined in that
living tomb which we carry about, now that we are imprisoned
in the body, as in an oyster-shell. Let me linger thus long over
the memory of scenes which have passed away.

But of beauty, I repeat again that we saw her there shining
in the company with the celestial forms; and coming to earth
d   we find her here too, shining in clearness through the clearest
aperture of sense. For sight is the keenest of our bodily senses;
though not by that is wisdom seen, for her loveliness would
have been transporting if there had been a visible image of her,
and this is true of the loveliness of the other ideas as well. But
beauty only has this portion, that she is once the loveliest and

also the most apparent. Now he who has not been lately ini-   e
tiated or who has become corrupted, is not easily carried out
of this world to the sight of absolute beauty in the other; he
looks only at that which has the name of beauty in this world,
and instead of being awed at the sight of her, like a brutish
beast he rushes on to enjoy[1] and beget; he takes wantonness
to his bosom, and is not afraid or ashamed of pursuing pleasure
in violation of nature. But he whose initiation is recent, and   251
who has been the spectator of many glories in the other world,
is amazed when he sees anyone having a god-like face or form,
which is the expression or imitation of divine beauty; and at
first a shudder runs through him, and some "misgiving" of a
former world steals over him; then looking upon the face of
his beloved as of a god he reverences him, and if he were not
afraid of being thought a downright madman, he would sacrifice to his beloved as to the image of a god; then as he gazes
on him there is a sort of reaction, and the shudder naturally
passes into an unusual heat and perspiration; for, as he receives   b
the effluence of beauty through the eyes, the wing moistens and
he warms. And as he warms, the parts out of which the wing
grew, and which had been hitherto closed and rigid, and had
prevented the wing from shooting forth are melted, and as
nourishment streams upon him, the lower end[2] of the wing
begins to swell and grow from the root upwards, extending under
the whole soul—for once the whole was winged. Now during   c
this process the whole soul is in a state of effervescence [is boiling,
or seething, and gushing forth] and irritation, like the state of
irritation and pain in the gums at the time of cutting teeth;
in like manner the soul [of the man] when beginning to grow
wings has inflammation [is seething], and pains and ticklings,
and when looking at the beauty of youth she receives the sensible warm traction of particles which flow towards her, therefore
called attraction (*himeros*), and is refreshed and warmed by them,
and then she ceases from her pain with joy. But when she is   d
separated and her moisture fails, then the orifices of the pas-

---

[1. Rather, "to mount" (as a stallion would a mare)]
[2. Rather, "the stalk" of the wing. The image seems more that of a winged arrow.]

sages out of which the wing shoots dry up and close, and inter-
cept the germ of the wing; which, being shut up within in company with desire, throbbing as with the pulsations of an artery,
pricks the aperture which is nearest, until at length the entire
soul is pierced and maddened and pained, and at the recollection of beauty is again delighted. And from both of them together the soul is oppressed at the strangeness of her condition,
e   and is in a great strait and excitement, and in her madness can
neither sleep by night nor abide in her place by day. And wherever she thinks that she will behold the beautiful one, thither
in her desire she runs. And when she has seen him, and drunk
rivers of desire, her constraint is loosened, and she is refreshed,
and has no more pangs and pains; and this is the sweetness
252 of all pleasures at the time, and is the reason why the soul of
the lover never forsakes his beautiful one, whom he esteems
above all; he has forgotten his mother and brethren and companions, and he thinks nothing of the neglect and loss of his
property; and as to the rules and proprieties of life, on which
he formerly prided himself, he now despises them, and is ready
to sleep and serve, wherever he is allowed, as near as he can
to his beautiful one who is not only the object of his worship,
b   but the only physician who can heal him in his extreme agony.
And this state, my dear imaginary youth, is by men called love,
and among the gods has a name which you, in your simplicity, may be inclined to mock; there are two lines in honor of
love in the Homeric Apocrypha in which the name occurs. One
of them is rather outrageous, and is not quite metrical; they
are as follow:—

> Mortals call him Eros (love),
> But the immortals call him Pteros (fluttering dove),
> Because fluttering of wings is a necessity to him.[1]

c   You may believe this or not as you like. At any rate the loves
of lovers and their causes are such as I have described.
   Now the lover who is the attendant of Zeus is better able

Love on
earth

is

imitation

of love
in heaven

[1. Literally, "Mortals call Love winged; immortals call him Feathered,
because he is constrained to grow feathers."]

to bear the winged god, and can endure a heavier burden; but the attendants and companions of Ares,[1] when under the influence of love, if they fancy that they have been at all wronged, are ready to kill and put an end to themselves and their beloved. And in like manner he who follows in the train of any other god honors him, and imitates him as far as he is able while the impression lasts; and this is his way of life and the manner of his behavior to his beloved and to every other in the first period of his earthly existence. Everyone chooses the object of his affections according to his character, and this he makes his god, and fashions and adorns as a sort of image which he is to fall down and worship. The followers of Zeus desire that their beloved should have a soul like him; and, therefore, they seek some philosophical and imperial nature, and when they have found him and loved him, they do all they can to create such a nature in him, and if they have no experience hitherto, they learn of anyone who can teach them, and themselves follow in the same way. And they have the less difficulty in finding the nature of their own god in themselves, because they have been compelled to gaze intensely on him; their recollection clings to him, and they become possessed by him, and receive his character and ways, as far as man can participate in God. These they attribute to the beloved, and they love him all the more, and if they draw inspiration from Zeus, like the Bacchic Nymphs, they pour this out upon him in order to make him as like their god as possible. But those who are the followers of Hera[2] seek a royal love, and when they have found him they do the same with him; and in like manner the followers of Apollo, and of every other god walking in the ways of their god, seek a love who is to be like their god, and when they have found him, they themselves imitate their god, and persuade their love to do the same, and bring him into harmony with the form and ways of the god as far as they can; for they have no feelings of envy or mean enmity towards their beloved, but they do their utmost to create in him the greatest likeness of themselves and the god whom they honor. And the desire

d

e

253

b

c

[1. The god of war]
[2. The wife of Zeus and queen of the gods]

of the lover, if effected, and the initiation of which I speak into the mysteries of true love, is thus fair and blissful to the beloved when he is chosen by the lover who is driven mad by love. Now the beloved or chosen one is taken captive in the following manner:—

As I said at the beginning of this tale, I divided each soul into three parts, two of them having the forms of horses and
d the third that of a charioteer; and one of the horses was good and the other bad, but I have not yet explained the virtue and vice of either, and to that I will now proceed. The well-conditioned horse is erect and well-formed; he has a lofty neck and an aquiline nose, and his color is white, and he has dark eyes and is a lover of honor and modesty and temperance, and the follower of true glory; he needs not the touch of the whip, but
e is guided by word and admonition only. Whereas the other is a large misshapen animal, put together anyhow; he has a strong short neck; he is flat-faced and of a dark color, grey-eyed and bloodshot, the mate of insolence and pride, shag-eared, deaf, hardly yielding to blow or spur. Now when the charioteer beholds the vision of love, and has his whole soul warmed with
254 sense, and is full of tickling and desire, the obedient steed then as always under the government of shame, refrains himself from leaping on the beloved; but the other, instead of heeding the blows of the whip, prances away and gives all manner of trouble to his companion and to the charioteer, and urges them on toward the beloved and reminds them of the joys of love. They at first indignantly oppose him and will not be urged on
b to do terrible and unlawful deeds; but at last, when there is no end of evil, they yield and suffer themselves to be led on to do as he bids them. And now they are at the spot and behold the flashing beauty of the beloved. But when the charioteer sees that, his memory is carried to the true beauty, and he beholds her in company with Modesty set in her holy place. And when he[1] sees her he is afraid and falls back in adoration, and in falling is compelled to pull back the reins, which he does with
c such force as to bring both the steeds on their haunches, the

---

[1. In Burnet's text, the subject is a feminine noun, i.e., the memory (of the charioteer).]

one willing and unresisting, the unruly one very unwilling; and
when they have gone back a little, the one is overflowing with
shame and wonder, and pours forth rivers of perspiration over
the entire soul; the other, when the pain is over which the bridle
and the fall had given him, having with difficulty taken breath,
is full of wrath and reproaches, which he heaps upon the charioteer and his fellow steed, as though from want of courage and
manhood they had been false to their agreement and guilty of
desertion. And, when they again decline, he forces them on,   d
and will scarce yield to their request that he would wait until
another time. Returning at the appointed hour, they make as
if they had forgotten, and he reminds them, fighting and neigh-
ing and dragging them, until at length he on the same thoughts
intent, forces them to draw near. And when they are near he
stoops his head and puts up his tail, and takes the bit in his
mouth and pulls shamelessly. Then the charioteer is worse off   e
than ever; he drops at the very start, and with still greater violence draws the bit out of the teeth of the wild steed and covers
his abusive tongue and jaws with blood, and forces his legs and
haunches to the ground and punishes him sorely. And when
this has happened several times and the villain has ceased from
his wanton way, he is tamed and humbled, and follows the will
of the charioteer, and when he sees the beautiful one he is ready
to die of fear. And from that time forward the soul of the lover
follows the beloved in modesty and holy fear.

   And so the beloved who, like a god, has received every true   255
and loyal service from his lover, not in pretense but in reality,
being also himself of a nature friendly to his admirer, if in former days he has blushed to his own passion and turned away
his lover, because his youthful companions or others slander-
ously told him that he would be disgraced, now as years advance,
at the appointed age and time is led to receive him into communion. For fate which has ordained that there shall be no   b
friendship among the evil has also ordained that there shall ever
be friendship among the good. And when he has received him
into communion and intimacy, then the beloved is amazed at
the good will of the lover; he recognizes that the inspired friend
is worth all other friendship or kinships, which have nothing of
friendship in them in comparison. And as he continues to feel

this and approaches and embraces him, in gymnastic exercises
and at other times of meeting, then does the fountain of that

c   stream, which Zeus when he was in love with Ganymede[1] called
desire, overflow upon the lover, and some enters into his soul,
and some when he is filled flows out again, and as a breeze
or an echo leaps from the smooth rocks and rebounds to them
again, so does the stream of beauty, passing the eyes which are
the natural doors and windows of the soul, return again to the

d   beautiful one; there arriving and fluttering the passages of the
wings, and watering them and inclining them to grow, and fill-
ing the soul of the beloved also with love. And thus he loves,
but he knows not what; he does not understand and cannot explain his own state; he appears to have caught the infection of
another's eye; the lover is his mirror in whom he is beholding
himself, but he is not aware of this. When he is with the lover,
both cease from their pain, but when he is away then he longs
as he is lonnged for, and has love's image, love for love (Anteros)

e   lodging in his breast, which he calls and deems not love but
friendship only, and his desire is as the desire of the other, but
weaker; he wants to see him, touch him, kiss, embrace him [go
to bed with him], and not long afterwards his desire is accomplished. Now, when they meet, the wanton steed of the lover
has a word to say to the charioteer; he would like to have a
little pleasure as a return for many pains, but the wanton steed

256 of the beloved says not a word, for he is bursting [swelling] with
passion which he understands not, but he throws his arms round
the lover and embraces him as his dearest friend; and, when they
are side by side [when they go to bed together], he is not in
a state in which he can refuse the lover anything, if he ask him,
while his fellow steed and the charioteer oppose him with shame
and reason. After this their happiness depends upon their self-
control;[2] if the better elements of the mind which lead to order

b   and philosophy prevail, then they pass their life in this world
in happiness and harmony—masters of themselves and orderly
—enslaving the vicious and emancipating the virtuous elements;

[1. The boy Ganymede was carried to heaven by Zeus, disguised as an
eagle, to be the god's cupbearer.]

[2. "After this their happiness . . . control" is not in the Greek text.]

and when the end comes, being light and ready to fly away, they conquer in one of the three heavenly or truly Olympian victories; nor can human discipline or divine inspiration confer any greater blessings on man than this. If, on the other hand, they leave philosophy and lead the lower life of ambition, then, probably in the dark [in their cups] or in some other careless hour, the two wanton animals take the two souls when off their guard and bring them together, and they accomplish that desire of their hearts which to the many is bliss; and thus having once enjoyed they continue to enjoy, yet rarely because they have not the approval of the whole soul. They too are dear, but not so dear to one another as the others, either at the time of their love or afterwards. They consider that they have given and taken from each other the most sacred pledges, and they may not break them and fall into enmity. At last they pass out of the body, unwinged, but eager to soar, and thus obtain no mean reward of love and madness. For those who have once begun the heavenward pilgrimage may not go down again to darkness and the journey beneath the earth, but they live in light always; happy companions in their pilgrimage, and when the time comes at which they receive their wings they have the same plumage because of their love.

Thus great are the heavenly blessings which the friendship of a lover will confer on you, my youth. Whereas the attachment of the non-lover which is just a vulgar compound of temperance and niggardly earthly ways and motives, will breed meanness—praised by the vulgar as virtue in your inmost soul; will send you bowling round the earth during a period of nine thousand years, and leave you a fool in the world below.

And thus, dear Eros, I have made and paid my recantation, as well as I could and as fairly as I could; the poetical figures I was compelled to use, because Phaedrus would have them. And now forgive the past and accept the present, and be gracious and merciful to me, and do not deprive me of sight[1] or take from me the art of love, but grant that I may be yet more esteemed in the eyes of the fair. And if Phaedrus or I myself said anything objectionable in our first speeches, blame

c

d

e

257

b

[1. Rather, "do not maim or mutilate me."]

Lysias, who is the father of the brat, and let us have no more of his progeny; bid him study philosophy, like his brother Polemarchus; and then his lover Phaedrus will no longer halt between two, but dedicate himself wholly to love and philosophical discourses.

Phaedr. I say with you, Socrates, may this come true if this be for my good. But why did you make this discourse of yours

c   so much finer than the other? I wonder at that. And I begin to be afraid that I shall lose conceit of Lysias, even if he be willing to make another as long as yours, which I doubt. For one of our politicians lately took to abusing him on this very account; he would insist on calling him a speech-writer. So that a feelingo of pride may probably induce him to give up writing.

Soc. That is an amusing notion; but I think that you are

d   a little mistaken in your friend if you imagine that he is frightened at every noise; and, possibly, you think that his assailant was in earnest?

Phaedr. I thought, Socrates, that he was. And you are aware that the most powerful and considerable men among our statesmen are ashamed of writing speeches and leaving them in a written form because they are afraid of posterity, and do not like to be called sophists.

Soc. I don't know whether you are aware, Phaedrus, that the "sweet elbow"[1] of which the proverb speaks is really derived

e   from the long and difficult arm of the Nile. And you appear to be equally unaware of the fact that this sweet elbow of theirs is also a long arm. For there is nothing of which great politicians are so fond as of writing speeches, which they bequeath to posterity. And when they write them, out of gratitude to their admirers, they append their names at the top.

Phaedr. What do you mean? I don't understand.

258   *Soc.* Why, don't you know that when a politician writes, he begins with the names of his approvers?

Phaedr. How is that?

Soc. Why, he begins thus: "Be it enacted by the senate, the people, or both, as a certain person who was the author

---

1. A proverb, like "the grapes are sour," applied to pleasures which cannot be had, meaning sweet things which are out of the reach of the mouth.

proposed"; and then he rehearses all his titles, and proceeds to display his own wisdom to his admirers with a great flourish in what is often a long and tedious composition. Now what is that sort of thing but a regular piece of authorship?

Phaedr. True.   258b

Soc. And if the law is passed, then, like the poet, he leaves the theater in high delight; but if the law is rejected and he is done out of his speech-making, and not thought good enough to write, then he and his party are in mourning.

Phaedr. Very true.

Soc. This shows how far they are from despising, or rather how highly they value the practice of writing.

Phaedr. No doubt.

Soc. And when the king or orator has the power, as Lycurgus[1] or Solon[2] or Darius[3] had, of attaining an immortality   c
of authorship in a state, is he not thought by posterity, when they see his writings, and does he not think himself, while he is yet alive, to be like a god?

Phaedr. That is true.

Soc. Then do you think that anyone of this class who may be ill-disposed to Lysias would ever make it a reproach against him that he is an author?

Phaedr. Not upon your view; for according to you he would be reproaching him with his own favorite pursuit.

Soc. Anyone may see that there is no disgrace in the fact   d
of writing?

Phaedr. Certainly not.

Soc. There may however be a disgrace in writing, not well, but badly.

Phaedr. That is true.

Soc. And what is well and what is badly—need we ask Lysias, or any other poet or orator, who ever wrote or will write either a political or any other work, in meter or out of meter, poet or prose writer, to teach us this?

Phaedr. Need we? What motive has a man to live if not   e

[1. The traditional founder of the Spartan constitution and military system]
[2. Athenian statesman and poet]
[3. The Persian king]

for the pleasure of discourse? Surely he would not live for the sake of bodily pleasures, which almost always have previous pain as a condition of them, and therefore are rightly called slavish.

Soc. There is time yet. And I can fancy that the grasshoppers who are still chirruping in the sun over our heads are talking to 259 one another and looking at us. What would they say if they saw that we also, like the many, are not talking but slumbering at mid-day, lulled by their voices, too indolent to think? They would have a right to laugh at us, and might imagine that we are slaves coming to our place of resort, who like sheep lie asleep at noon about the fountain. But if they see us discoursing, and like Odysseus sailing by their siren voices, they may perhaps, out of respect, give b us of the gifts which they receive of the gods and give to men.

Phaedr. What gifts do you mean? I never heard of any.

Soc. A lover of music like yourself ought surely to have heard the story of the grasshoppers, who are said to have been human beings in an age before the Muses. And when the Muses came and song appeared they were ravished with delight; and c singing always, never thought of eating and drinking, until at last they forgot and died. And now they live again in the grass-hoppers; and this is the return which the Muses make to them —they hunger no more, neither thirst any more, but are always singing from the moment that they are born, and never eating or drinking; and when they die they go and inform the Muses in heaven who honors them on earth. They win the love of Terpischore for the dancers by their report of them; of Erato d for the lovers, and of the other Muses for those who do them honor, according to the several ways of honoring them;—of Calliope the eldest Muse, and of her who is next to her for the votaries of philosophy; for these are the Muses who are chiefly concerned with heaven and the ideas, divine as well as human, and they have the sweetest utterance. For many reasons, then, we ought always to talk and not to sleep at mid-day.

Phaedr. Let us talk.

e *Soc.* Shall we discuss the rules of writing and speech as we were proposing?

Phaedr. Very good.

Soc. Is not the first rule of good speaking that the mind of the speaker should know the truth of what he is going to say?

Phaedr. And yet, Socrates, I have heard that he who would
be an orator has nothing to do with true justice, but only with
that which is likely to be approved by the many who sit in
judgment; nor with the truly good or honorable, but only with
public opinion about them, and that from this source and not
from the truth come the elements of persuasion.

Soc. Any words of the wise ought to be regarded and not
trampled underfoot, for there is probably something in them, and
perhaps there may be something in this which is worthy of attention.

Phaedr. Very true.

Soc. Let us put the matter thus;—Suppose that I persuaded
you to buy a horse and go to the wars. Neither of us know
what a horse was like, but I knew that you believed a horse
to be the longest-eared of domestic animals.

Phaedr. That would be ridiculous.

Soc. There is something more ridiculous coming. Suppose,
now, that I was in earnest and went and composed a speech in
honor of an ass, whom I entitled a horse, beginning: "A noble
animal and a most useful possession, especially in war, and you
may get on his back and fight, and he will carry baggage or anything."

Phaedr. That would be most ridiculous.

Soc. Ridiculous! Yes; but is not even a ridiculous friend
better than a dangerous enemy?

Phaedr. Certainly.

Soc. And when the orator instead of putting an ass in the
place of a horse, puts good for evil, being himself as ignorant
of their true nature as the city on which he imposes is ignorant; and having studied the notions of the mulititude, persuades
them to do evil instead of good,—what will be the harvest which
rhetoric will be likely to gather after the sowing of that fruit?

Phaedr. Anything but good.

Soc. Perhaps, however, rhetoric has been getting too rough-
ly handled by us, and she might answer: What amazing nonsense is this! As if I forced any man to learn to speak in igno-
ance of the truth! Whatever my advice may be worth, I should
have told him to arrive at the truth first, and then come to
me. At the same time I boldly assert that mere knowledge of
the truth will not give you the art of persuasion.

Phaedr. There is reason in the lady's defense of herself.

260

b

c

d

e

Soc. Yes, I admit that, if the argument which she has yet in store bear witness that she is an art at all. But I seem to hear them arraying themselves on the opposite side, declaring that she speaks not true, and that rhetoric is not an art but only a dillettante amusement. Lo! a Spartan appears, and says that there never is nor ever will be a real art of speaking which is unconnected with the truth.

261   *Phaedr.* And what are these arguments? Socrates? Bring them out that we may examine them.

Soc. Come out, children of my soul, and convince Phaedrus who is the father of similar beauties, that he will never be able to speak about anything unless he be trained in philosophy. And let Phaedrus answer you.

Phaedr. Put the question.

Soc. Is not rhetoric, taken generally, a universal art of enchanting the mind by arguments; which is practiced not only in courts and public assemblies, but in private houses also, having to do with all matters, great as well as small, good and bad alike, and is in all equally right, and equally to be esteemed

b   —that is what you have heard?

Phaedr. Nay, not exactly that; but I should rather say that I have heard the art confined to speaking and writing in lawsuits, and to speaking in public assemblies—not extended farther.

Soc. Then I suppose that you have only heard of the rhetoric of Nestor and Odysseus, which they composed in their leisure hours when at Troy, and never of Palamedes?[1]

c   *Phaedr.* No more than of Nestor and Odysseus, unless Gorgias[2] is your Nestor, and Thrasymachus[3] and Theodorus[4] your Odysseus.

[1. Palamedes means "the handy or contriving one." His chief distinctions were his invention of letters and his cunning while serving under Agamemnon, commander-in-chief of the Greek expedition against Troy.]

[2. Gorgias, ca. 483–376 B.C. Greek sophist and rhetorician. Gorgias aimed at an "artistic" prose style that would rival poetry in its effect.]

[3. Thrasymachus (fl. ca. 430–400 B.C.) was a sophist and rhetorician who played an important role in the development of Greek oratory. He is best known for his defense, in the *Republic*, of the thesis that justice is in the interest of the stronger.]

[4. A mathematician and teacher of Plato (b. ca. 460 B.C.)]

Soc. Perhaps that is my meaning. But let us leave them. And do you tell me, instead, what are plaintiff and defendant doing in a law-court—are they not contending?

Phaedr. Exactly.

Soc. About the just and unjust—that is the matter in dispute?

Phaedr. Yes.

Soc. And he who is practiced in the art will make the same thing appear to the same persons to be at one time just and at another time unjust, if he has a mind?

d

Phaedr. Exactly.

Soc. And when he speaks in the assembly, he will make the same things seem good to the city at one time, and at another time the reverse of good?

Phaedr. That is true.

Soc. Have we not heard of the Eleatic Palamedes (Zeno),[1] who has an art of speaking which makes the same things appear to his hearers like and unlike, one and many, at rest and in motion too?

Phaedr. Very true.

Soc. The art of disputation, then, is not confined to the courts and the assembly, but is one and the same in every use of language; this is that art, if such an art there be, which finds a likeness of everything to which a likeness can be found, and draws into the light of day the likenesses and disguises which are used by others?

e

Phaedr. How do you mean?

Soc. Let me put the matter thus: When will there be more chance of deception—when the difference is large or small?

Phaedr. When the difference is small.

262

Soc. And you will be less likely to be discovered in passing by degrees into the other extreme than when you go all at once?

Phaedr. Of course.

Soc. He, then, who would deceive others, and not be deceived, must exactly know the real likenesses and differences of things?

Phaedr. Yes, he must.

Soc. And if he is ignorant of the true nature of anything, how can he ever distinguish the greater or less degree of likeness to other things of that which he does not know?

[1. Zeno of Elea, b. ca. 490 B.C.]

b   *Phaedr.* He cannot.

Soc. And when men are deceived, and their notions are at variance with realities, it is clear that the error slips in through some resemblances?

Phaedr. Yes, that is the way.

Soc. Then he who would be a master of the art must know the real nature of everything; or he will never know either how to contrive or how to escape the gradual departure from truth into the opposite of truth which is effected by the help of resemblances?

Phaedr. He will not.

c   *Soc.* He then, who being ignorant of the truth catches at appearances, will only attain an art of rhetoric which is ridiculous and is not an art at all?

Phaedr. That may be expected.

Soc. Shall I propose that we look for examples of good and bad art, according to our notion of them, in the speech of Lysias which you have in your hand, and in my own speech?

Phaedr. Nothing could be better; and indeed I think that our previous argument has been too barren of illustrations.

Soc. Yes; and the two speeches afford a good illustration
d   of the way in which the speaker who knows the truth may playfully draw away the hearts of his hearers. This piece of good fortune I attribute to the local deities; and, perhaps, the prophets of the Muses who are singing over our heads may have imparted their inspiration to me. For I do not imagine that I have any rehetorical art myself.

Phaedr. I will not dispute that; only please to go forward.

Soc. Suppose that you read me the first words of Lysias' speech?

e   *Phaedr.* "You know my views of our common interest, and I do not think that I ought to fail in the object of my suit because I am not your lover. For lovers repent when—"

Soc. Enough. Now, shall I point out the rhetorical error of these words?

263   *Phaedr.* Yes.

Soc. Everyone is aware that about some things we are agreed, whereas about other things we differ.

Phaedr. I think that I understand you; but will you explain yourself?

Soc. When anyone speaks of iron and silver, is not the same thing present in the minds of all?

Phaedr. Certainly.

Soc. But when anyone speaks of justice and goodness, there is every sort of disagreement, and we are at odds with one another and with ourselves?

Phaedr. Precisely.

Soc. Then in some things we agree, but not in others? 263b

Phaedr. That is true.

Soc. In which are we more likely to be deceived, and in which has rhetoric the greater power?

Phaedr. Clearly, in the class which admits of error.

Soc. Then the rhetorician ought to make a regular division, and acquire a distinct notion of both classes, as well of that in which the many err, as of that in which they do not err?

Phaedr. He who made such a distinction would have an c excellent principle.

Soc. Yes; and in the next place he must have a keen eye for the observation of particulars in speaking, and not make a mistake about the class to which they are to be referred.

Phaedr. Certainly.

Soc. Now to which class does love belong—to the debatable or to the undisputed class?

Phaedr. To the debatable class surely; for if not, do you think that anyone would have allowed you to say as you did, that love is an evil both to the lover and the beloved, and also the greatest possible good?

Soc. Capital. But will you tell me whether I defined love d at the beginning of my speech? For, having been in an ecstasy, I cannot well remember.

Phaedr. Yes, indeed; that you did, and no mistake.

Soc. Then I perceive that the Nymphs of Achelous and Pan the Son of Hermes, who inspired me, were far better rhetoricians than Lysias the son of Cephalus. Alas! How inferior to them he is! But perhaps I am mistaken; and Lysias at the commencement of his lover's speech did insist on our supposing love to be something or other which he fancied him to be, and that in relation to this something he fashioned and framed the e remainder of his discourse. Suppose we read him over again.

Phaedr. If you please; but you will not find what you want.

Soc. Read, that I may have his exact words.

Phaedr. "You know my views of our common interest; and I do not think that I ought to fail in the object of my suit because I am not your lover, for lovers repent of the kindnesses which they have shown, when their love is over."

264

Soc. Here he appears to have done just the reverse of what he ought; for he has begun at the end, and is swimming on his back through the flood of words to the place of starting. His address to the fair youth commences with reference to the conclusion of his love. Am I not right, sweet Phaedrus?

b

Phaedr. Yes, indeed, Socrates; he does begin at the end.

Soc. Then as to the other topics—are they not a mass of confusion? Is there any principle in them? Why should the next topic or any other topic follow in that order? I cannot help fancying in my ignorance that he wrote freely off just what came into his head, but I dare say that you would recognize a rhetorical necessity in the succession of the several parts of the composition?

c

Phaedr. You have too good an opinion of me if you think that I have any such insight into his principles of composition.

Soc. At any rate, you will allow that every discourse ought to be a living creature, having its own body and head and feet; there ought to be a middle, beginning, and end, which are in a manner agreeable to one another and to the whole?

Phaedr. Certainly.

Soc. Can this be said of the discourse of Lysias? See whether you can find any more connections in his words than in the epitaph, which is said by some to have been inscribed on the grave of Midas the Phrygian.

d

Phaedr. What is there remarkable in the epitaph?

Soc. The epitaph is as follows:

> I am a maiden of brass;
> I lie on the tomb of Midas,
> While waters flow and tall trees grow,
>   Here am I.
> On Midas' tearful tomb I lie;
> I am to tell the passers by
> That Midas sleeps in earth below.

Now in this rhyme whether a line comes first or comes last,   e
that, as you will perceive, makes no difference.

Phaedr. You are making fun of that oration of ours.

Soc. Well, I will say no more about your friend lest I should
give offense to you; although I think that he might furnish many
other examples of what a man ought to avoid. But I will proceed
to the other speech, which, as I think, is also suggestive to students
of rhetoric.

Phaedr. In what way?   265

Soc. The two speeches, as you may remember, were of an
opposite character, the one argued that the lover and the other
that the non-lover ought to be accepted.

Phaedr. And right manfully.

Soc. You should rather say "madly"; and that was the argument of them, for, as I said, "love is a madness."

Phaedr. Yes.

Soc. And there were two kinds of madness; one produced
by human infirmity, the other by a divine release from the ordinary
ways of men.

Phaedr. True.   b

Soc. The divine madness was subdivided into four kinds,
prophetic, initiatory, poetic, erotic, having four gods presiding over
them; the first was the inspiration of Apollo, the second that of
Dionysus, the third that of the Muses, the fourth that of Aphrodite
and Eros. In the description of the last kind of madness, which
was also the best, being a sort of figure of love, we mingled a
tolerably credible and possibly true, though partly erring myth,
which was also a hymn in honor of Eros, who is your lord and   c
also mine, Phaedrus, and the guardian of fair children, and to
him we sang the hymn in measured and solemn form.

Phaedr. I know that I had great pleasure in listening to
the tale.

Soc. Let us take this instance and examine how the transition
was made from blame to praise.

Phaedr. What do you mean?

Soc. I mean to say that the composition was mostly playful.
Yet in these chance fancies of the hour were involved two principles which would be charming if they could be fixed by art.   d

Phaedr. What are they?

Soc. First, the comprehension of scattered particulars in one idea;—the speaker defines his several notions in order that he may make his meaning clear, as in our definition of love, which whether true or false certainly gave clearness and consistency to the discourse.

Phaedr. What is the other principle, Socrates?

Soc. Secondly, there is the faculty of division according to the natural ideas or members, not breaking any part as a bad carver[1] might. But, as the body may be divided into a left side and into a right side, having parts right and left, so in the two discourses there was assumed, first of all, the general idea of unreason, and then one of the two proceeded to divide the parts of the left side and did not desist until he found in them an evil or left-handed love which the speaker justly reviled; and the other leading us to the right portion in which madness lay, found another love, having the same name, but yet divine, which he held up before us and applauded as the author of the greatest benefits.

Phaedr. That is most true.

Soc. I am a great lover of these processes of division and generalization; they help me to speak and think. And if I find any man who is able to see unity and plurality in nature, him I follow, and walk in his step as if he were a god. And those who have this art, I have hitherto been in the habit of calling dialecticians; but God knows whether the name is right or not. And I should like to know what name you would give to your or Lysias' disciples, and whether this may not be that famous art of rhetoric which Thrasymachus and others practice? Skillful speakers they are, and impart their skill to anyone who will consent to worship them as kings and to bring them gifts.

Phaedr. Yes, they are royal men; but their art is not the same with the art of those whom you call, and rightly, in my opinion, dialecticians. Still we are in the dark about rhetoric.

Soc. What do you mean? The remains of the art, when all this has been taken away, must be of rare value; and are not at all to be despised by you and me. But what are the remains?—tell me that.

[1. I.e., a carver of meat, a butcher]

Phaedr. There is a great deal surely to be found in the books of rhetoric?

Soc. Yes; thank you for reminding me of that, there is the prooemium, if I remember rightly—that is what you mean—the niceties of the art?

Phaedr. Yes.

e

Soc. There follows the statement of facts, and upon that witnesses; thirdly, proofs; fourthly, probabilities are to come; the great Byzantian artist also speaks, if I am not mistaken, of confirmation and superconfirmation.

Phaedr. You mean the excellent Theodorus.

Soc. Yes; and he tells how refutation or further refutation is to be managed, whether in accusation or defense. I need hardly mention the Parian Evenus,[1] who first invented indirect allusions and incidental praises, and also censures, of which this wise man made a *memoria technica* in verse. But shall

267

> I to dumb forgetfulness consign

Tisias[2] and Gorgias, who are not ignorant that probability is superior to truth, and who by force of argument make the little appear great and the great little, and the new old and the old new, and have discovered universal forms, either short or going on to infinity. I remember Prodicus laughing when I told him of this; he said that he had himself discovered the true rule of art, which was to be neither long nor short, but of a convenient length.

b

Phaedr. Well, done, Prodicus.

Soc. Then there is Hippias of Elis,[3] who probably agrees with him.

Phaedr. Yes.

Soc. And there is also Polus,[4] who has schools of diplasiology,[5] and gnomology, and eikonology, and who teaches in

c

[1. Fifth-century B.C. poet and sophist]

[2. Tisias of Syracuse (fifth century B.C.): teacher of Gorgias and Isocrates]

[3. Fl. fifth century B.C. He acquired great fame and wealth by traveling around Greece as a teacher and orator.]

[4. Sophist, younger contemporary of Socrates]

[5. In rhetoric, the study of the word repetition for the sake of emphasis]

them the words of which Licymnius[1] made him a present; they were to give a polish.

Phaedr. Had not Protagoras something of the same sort?

Soc. Yes, rules of correctness and many other fine precepts; for the "sorrows of a poor old man," or any other pathetic case, no one is better than the Chalcedonian giant;[2] he can put a

d   whole company of people into a passion and out of one again by his might magic, and is first-rate at inventing or disposing of any sort of calumny on any grounds or none. All of them agree in asserting that a speech should end in a recapitulation, though they do not all agree in the use of this word.

Phaedr. You mean that there should be a summing up of the arguments in order to remind the hearers of them.

Soc. I have now said all that I have to say of the art of rhetoric: have you anything to add?

Phaedr. Not much, nor very important.

268   ✳ *Soc.* Leave the unimportant and let us bring the really important question into the light of day, which is: What power this art of rhetoric has, and when?

Phaedr. A very great power in public meetings.

Soc. Yes, that is true. But I should like to know whether you have the same feeling as I have about the rhetoricians? To me there seems to be a great many holes in their web.

Phaedr. Give an example.

Soc. I will. Suppose a person to come to your friend Eryximachus, or to his father Acumenus, and say to him: "I know how to apply drugs which shall have either a heating or a cooling

b   effect, and I can give a vomit and also a purge, and all that sort of thing; and knowing all this, as I do, I claim to be a physician and a teacher of physic"—what do you suppose that they would say?

Phaedr. They would be sure to ask him whether he knew "to whom" he would give them, and "when," and "how much."

Soc. And suppose that he were to reply? "No; I know nothing of that; I expect those whom I have taught all this to do that

c   of themselves."

[1. Licymnius of Chios: dithyrambic poet and rhetorician, teacher of Polus]
[2. I.e., Thrasymachus]

Phaedr. They would reply that he is a madman or a pedant who fancies that he is a physician, because he has read something in a book, or has stumbled on a few drugs, although he has no real understanding of the art of medicine.

Soc. And suppose a person were to come to Sophocles or Euripides and say that he knows how to make a long speech about a small matter, and a short speech about a great matter, and also a sorrowful speech, or a terrible, or threatening speech, or any other kind of speech, and in teaching this fancies that   d
he is teaching the art of tragedy?

Phaedr. They too would surely laugh at him if he fancies that tragedy is anything but the arranging of these elements in a manner suitable to one another and to the whole.

Soc. But I do not suppose that they would be rude to him or revile him. Would they not treat him as a musician would treat a man who thinks that he is a harmonist because he knows how to pitch the highest and lowest note; happening to meet   e
such an one he would not say to him savagely, "Fool, you are mad!"[1] Oh, no; he would rather say to him in a gentle and musical tone of voice: "My good friend, he who would be a harmonist must certainly know this, and yet he may understand nothing of harmony if he has not got beyond your stage of knowledge, for you only know the preliminaries of harmony and not harmonies."

Phaedr. Very true.

Soc. And would not Sophocles say to the display of the   269
would-be tragedian, that this was not tragedy but the preliminaries of tragedy, and would not Acumenus say to the would-be doctor that this was not medicine but the preliminaries of medicine?

Phaedr. Very true.

Phaedr. And if Adrastus the mellifluous or Pericles[2] heard of these wonderful arts, brachylogies[3] and eikonologies and all the hard names which we have been endeavoring to draw into the light of day, what would they say? Instead of losing temper and applying uncomplimentary epithets, as you and I have been   b

---

[1. The Greek word is *melancholais,* literally, "You are atrabilious."]

[2. Athenian statesman (ca. 495–429 B.C.)]

[3. I.e., brevities in speech or writing]

doing to the authors of such an imaginary art, their superior wisdom would rather censure us, as well as them. Have a little patience, Phaedrus and Socrates, they would say, and don't be angry with those who from some want of dialectical skill are unable to define the nature of rhetoric, and consequently suppose that they have found the art in the preliminary conditions of the art, and when they have taught these to others, fancy that

c　they have been teaching the whole art of rhetoric; but as to persuasion in detail and unity of composition, that they regard as an easy thing with which their disciples may supply themselves.

　　Phaedr. I quite admit, Socrates, that the art of rhetoric which these men teach and of which they write is such as you describe— in that I agree with you. But I still want to know where and

d　how the true art of rhetoric and persuasion is to be acquired.

　　Soc. The perfection of oratory is, or rather must be, like the perfection of all things, partly given by nature; but this is assisted by art, and if you have the natural power you will be famous as a rhetorician, if you only add knowledge and practice, and in either you may fall short. But the art, as far as there is an art, of rhetoric does not lie in the direction of Tisias or Thrasymachus.

　　Phaedr. But in what direction then?

e　　*Soc.* I should conceive that Pericles was the most ac- complished of rhetoricians.

　　Phaedr. What of that?

270　　*Soc.* All the higher arts require much discussion and lofty contemplation of nature; this is the source of sublimity and perfect comprehensive power. And this, as I conceive, was the quality which, in addition to his natural gifts, Pericles acquired from his happening to know Anaxagoras.[1] He was imbued with the higher philosophy, and attained the knowledge of mind and matter, which was the favorite theme of Anaxgoras, and hence he drew what was applicable to his art.

　　Phaedr. Explain.

[1. Greek philosopher (ca. 500–428 B.C.). He contended that all natural objects are a mixture of infinitesimally small particles containing mixtures of all qualities, and that mind or intelligence acts on masses of these particles to produce objects.]

Soc. Rhetoric is like medicine.　　　　　　　　　　　　　　b

Phaedr. How is that?

Soc. Why, because medicine has to define the nature of the body and rhetoric of the soul—if you would proceed, not empirically but scientifically, in the one case to impart health and strength by giving medicine and food, in the other to implant the conviction which you require by the right use of words and principles.

Phaedr. You are probably right in that.

Soc. And do you think that you can know the nature of　　c the soul intelligently without knowing the nature of the whole?

Phaedr. Hippocrates the Asclepiad[1] says that this is the only method of procedure by which the nature even of the body can be understood.

Soc. Yes, friend, and he says truly. Still, we ought not be content with the name of Hippocrates, but to examine and see whether he has reason on his side.

Phaedr. True.

Soc. Then consider what this is which Hippocrates says, and which right reason says about this or any other nature. Ought we not to consider first whether that which we wish either to learn or to teach is simple or multiform, and if simple, then to　　d inquire what power this has of acting or being acted upon by other, and if multiform, then to number the forms; and see first in the case of one of them, and then in the case of all of them, the several powers which they by nature have of doing or suffering.

Phaedr. That will be the way.

Soc. The method which has not this analysis is like the groping of a blind man. Yet, surely he who is an artist ought not to admit of a comparison with the blind, or deaf; but he　　e who imparts rules of speech in an artist-like or scientific manner will particularly set forth the nature of that to which he gives his rules, which I suppose is the soul.

Phaedr. Certainly.

Soc. His whole effort is directed towards this, for in this　　271 he seeks to produce conviction.

[1. Hippocrates (ca. 460–ca. 377 B.C.). Greek physician, known as the "Father of Medicine." He is called the Asclepiad because the god Asclepius was the patron deity of medicine.]

Phaedr. Yes.

Soc. Then clearly, Thrasymachus or any oneelse who elaborates a system of rhetoric will give an exact description of the nature of the soul; which he will make to appear either as single and same, or, like the body, multiform. That is what we should call showing the nature of soul.

Phaedr. Exactly.

Soc. He will next proceed to speak of the instruments by which the soul acts or is affected in any way.

Phaedr. True.

271b   *Soc.* Thirdly, having arranged men and speeches, and their modes and affections in different classes, and fitted them into one another, he will point out the connection between them—he will show why one is naturally persuaded by a particular form of argument, and another not.

Phaedr. That will certainly be a very good way.

Soc. Yes, that is the true and only way in which any subject can be set forth or treated by rules of art, whether in speaking c   or writing. But the writers of the present day, at whose feet you have sat, improperly conceal[1] all this about the soul which they know quite well. Nor, until they adopt our method of reading and writing, can we admit that they write by rules of art.

Phaedr. What is our method?

Soc. I cannot give you the exact details; but I should like to tell you generally, as far as I can, how a man ought to proceed according to the rules of art.

Phaedr. Let me hear.

Soc. Oratory is the art of enchanting the soul, and therefore d   he who would be an orator has to learn the differences of human souls—they are so many and of such a nature, and from them come the differences between man and man—he will then proceed to divide speeches into their different classes. Such and such persons, he will say, are affected by this or that kind of speech in this or that way, and he will tell you why; he must have a theoretical notion of them first, and then he must see them e   in action, and be able to follow them with all his senses about

---

[1. "Improperly conceal." Rather, "are villains (lit. "ready to do anything") in the arts of speaking and conceal . . .]

him, or he will never get beyond the precepts of his masters. But when he is able to say what persons are persuaded by what arguments, and recognize the individual about whom he used to theorize as actually present to him, and say to himself, "This is he and this is the sort of man who ought to have that argument applied to him in order to convince him of this";—when he has attained the knowledge of all this, and knows also when he should speak and when he should abstain from speaking, and when he should make use of pithy sayings, pathetic appeals, aggravated effects, and all the other figures of speech;—when, I say, he knows the times and seasons of all these things, then, and not till then, he is perfect and a consummate master of his art; but if he fail in any of these points, whether in speaking or teaching or writing them, and says that he speaks by rules of art, he who denies this has the better of him. Well, the teacher will say, is this Phaedrus and Socrates, your account of the art of rhetoric, or am I to look for another?

272

b

Phaedr. He must take this, Socrates, for there is no possibility of another, and yet the creation of such an art is not easy.

Soc. That is true; and therefore let us turn the matter up and down, and see whether there may not be a shorter and easier road; there is no use in taking the longer and more difficult way when there is a shorter and easier one. And I wish that you would try and remember whether there is anything which you have heard from Lysias or any one else which might be of service to us.

c

Phaedr. If trying would avail, then I might; but I fear that I cannot remember anything at the moment.

Soc. Suppose I tell you something which somebody who knows told me.

Phaedr. Certainly.

Soc. May not the wolf, as the proverb says, claim a hearing?

Phaedr. Do you say what can be said for him.

d

Soc. Well, they say that there is no use in putting a solemn face on a matter, or in going round and round, until you arrive at the beginning of all things; for that when the question is of justice and good, as I said at first, or a question in which men are concerned who are just and good, either by nature or habit, he who would be a skillful rhetorician has no need

of truth—for that in courts of law men literally care nothing
e about truth, but only about conviction: and this is based on
probability, to which he who would be a skillful orator should
therefore give his whole attention. And they say also that there
are cases in which the actual facts ought to be withheld, and
only the probabilities should be told either in accusation or
defense, and that always in speaking the orator should run after
probability, and say good-bye to the truth. And the observance
of this principle throughout a speech furnishes the whole art.

273 *Phaedr.* That is what the professors of rhetoric[1] actually
say, Socrates, for I remember that although we have touched
upon this matter but slightly, the point is all-important with them.

Soc. I dare say that you are familiar with Tisias. Does he
b not define probability to be that which the many think?

Phaedr. Certainly, he does.

Soc. I believe that he has a clever and ingenious case of this
sort:—He supposes a feeble and valiant man to have assaulted
a strong and cowardly one, and to have robbed him of his coat
or of something or other; he is brought into court, and then Tisias
says that both parties should tell lies; the coward should say that
he was assaulted by more men than one; the other should prove
c that they were alone, and should use this argument: "How could
a man like me have assaulted a man like him?" The other will
not like to confess his own cowardice, and will therefore invent
some other lie which his adversary will thus gain an opportunity
of refuting. These and others like them are the precepts of the
doctors of art. Am I not right, Phaedrus?

Phaedr. Certainly.

Soc. I cannot help feeling that this is a wonderfully mysterious
art which Tisias has discovered, or whoever the gentleman was,
or whatever his name or country may have been who was the
discoverer. Shall we say a word to him or not?

d *Phaedr.* What shall we say to him?

Soc. Let us tell him that, before he appeared, you and I
were saying that probability was engendered in the minds of
the many by the likeness of the truth, and were setting forth
that he who knew the truth would always know how best

[1. "Professors of rhetoric." literally, "those alleging to be skilled in
speaking"]

to discover the resemblances of the truth. If he has anything
further to say about the art of speaking we should like to hear
him; but if not, we are satisfied with our own view, [that unless
a man estimates the various characters of his hearers and is
able to divide existences into classes and to sum them up in   e
single ideas, he will never be a skillful rhetorician even within
the limits of human power.] And this art he will not attain without a great deal of trouble, which a good man ought to undergo, not for the sake of speaking and acting before men, but
in order that he may be able to say what is acceptable to God[1]
and in all things to act acceptably to Him as far as in him
lies; for there is a saying of wiser men than ourselves, that a
man of sense should not try to please his fellow servants (at
least this should not be his principle object) but his good and   274
noble masters, so that, if the way is long and circuitous, marvel
not at this; for, where the end is great, there the way may be
permitted to be long, but not for lesser ends such as yours.
Truly, the argument may say, Tisias, that if you do not mind
going so far, rhetoric has a fair beginning in this.

Phaedr. I think, Socrates, that this is admirable, if only
practicable.

Soc. But even to fail in an honorable object is honorable.   b

Phaedr. True.

Soc. I think that enough has been said of a true and false
art of speaking.

Phaedr. Certainly.

Soc. But there is something yet to be said of propriety and
impropriety of writing.

Phaedr. Yes.

Soc. Do you know how you can speak or act about rhetoric in a manner which will be acceptable to God?

Phaedr. No, indeed. Do you?

Soc. I have heard a tradition of antiquity, whether true or   c
not antiquity only knows. If we had the truth ourselves, do you
think that we should care much about the opinions of men?

Phaedr. That is a question which needs no answer; but I
wish that you would tell me what you say that you have heard.

[1. Rather "to the gods" and "acceptably to them . . ."]

Soc. At the Egyptian city of Naucratis, there was a famous old god, whose name was Theuth; the bird which is called the Ibis was sacred to him, and he was the inventor of many arts,

d such as arithmetic and calculation and geometry and draughts and dice, but his great discovery was the use of letters. Now in those days Thamus was the king of the whole of Upper Egypt, which is the district surrounding that great city which is called by the Hellenes Egyptian Thebes, and they call the god himself Ammon. To him came Theuth and showed his inventions, desiring that the other Egyptians might be allowed to have the benefit of them; he went through them, and Thamus inquired about their several uses, and praised some of them and censured

e others, as he approved or disapproved of them. There would be no use in repeating all that Thamus said to Theuth in praise or blame of the various arts. But when they came to letters, This, said Theuth, will make the Egyptians wiser and give them better memories; for this is the cure of forgetfulness and of folly. Thamus replied: O most ingenious Theuth, he who has the gift of invention is not always the best judge of the utility or inutility of his own inventions to the users of them. And in this in-

275 stance a paternal love of your own child has led you to say what is not the fact; for this invention of yours will create forgetfulness in the learners' souls, because they will not use their memories; they will trust to the external written characters and not remember of themselves. You have found a specific not for memory but for reminiscence, and you give your disciples only the pretense of wisdom; they will be hearers of many things and will have learned nothing; they will appear

b to be omniscient and will generally know nothing; they will be tiresome [to be with], having the reputation of knowledge without the reality.

Phaedr. Yes, Socrates, you can easily invent tales of Egypt, or of any other country that you like.

Soc. There was a tradition in the temple of Dodona that oaks first gave prophetic utterances. The men of that day, unlike in their simplicity to young philosophy, deemed that if they heard the truth even from "oak to rock," that was enough for them; whereas, you seem to think not of the truth but of the speaker,

c and of the country from which the truth comes.

Phaedr. I acknowledge the justice of your rebuke; and I think that the Theban is right in his view about letters.

Soc. He would be a simple person, and quite without understanding of the oracles Thamus and Ammon, who should leave in writing or receive in writing any art under the idea that the written word would be intelligible or certain; or who deemed that writing was at all better than knowledge and recollection of the same matters.

Phaedr. That is most true.

Soc. I cannot help feeling, Phaedrus, that writing is unfortunately like painting; for the creations of the painter have the attitude of life, and yet if you ask them a question they preserve a solemn silence. And the same may be said of speeches. You would imagine that they had intelligence, but if you want to know anything and put a question to one of them, the speaker always gives one unvarying answer. And when they have been once written down they are tossed about anywhere among those who do and among those who do not understand them. And they have no reticences or proprieties towards different classes of persons; and, if they are unjustly assailed or abused, their parent is needed to protect his offspring, for they cannot protect or defend themselves.

Phaedr. That again is most true.

Soc. May we not imagine another kind of writing or speaking far better than this is, and having far greater power—which is one of the same family, but lawfully begotten? Let us see what his origin is.

Phaedr. Who is he, and what do you mean about his origin?

Soc. I am speaking of an intelligent writing which is graven in the soul of him who has learned, and can defend itself, and know when to speak and when to be silent.

Phaedr. You mean the word of knowledge which has a living soul, and of which the written word is properly no more than an image?

Soc. Yes, of course that is what I mean. And I wish that you would let me ask you a question: Would a husbandman, who is a man of sense, take the seeds, which he values and which he wishes to be fruitful, and in sober earnest plant them

d

e

276

b

during the heat of summer, in some garden of Adonis,[1] that
he may rejoice when he sees them in eight days appearing in
beauty (at least he does that, if at all, only as the show of a
festival); but those about which he is in earnest he sows in fit-
ting soil, and practices husbandry, and is satisfied if in eight
months they arrive at perfection?

276c   *Phaedr.* Yes, Socrates, that will be his way when he is in
earnest; he will do the other, as you say, only as an amusement.

Soc. And can we suppose that he who knows the just and
good and honorable has less understanding in reference to his
own seeds than the husbandman?

Phaedr. Certainly not.

Soc. Then he will not seriously incline to write them in
water [sowing seed] with pen and ink or in dumb characters
which have not a word to say for themselves and cannot
adequately express the truth?

d   *Phaedr.* No, that is not likely.

Soc. No, that is not likely—in the garden of letters he will
plant them only as an amusement, or he will write them down
as memorials against the forgetfulness of old age, to be treasured
by him and his equals when they, like him, have one foot in
the grave; and he will rejoice in beholding their tender growth;
and they will be his pastime while others are watering the garden
of their souls with banqueting and the like.

Phaedr. A pastime, Socrates, as noble as the other is ignoble,
when a man is able to pass time merrily in the representation
of justice and the like.

e   *Soc.* True, Phaedrus. But nobler far is the serious pursuit
of the dialectician, who finds a congenial soul, and then with
knowledge engrafts and sows words which are able to help

[1. Adonis was a vegetation god who in mythology was portrayed as a
beautiful youth beloved by the goddess Aphrodite. In one mythical account,
Aphrodite concealed the infant Adonis in a box and entrusted the box to
Persephone, queen of the underworld, who refused to restore Adonis until
it was agreed that Adonis should spend part of each year on earth, part in
the world below. During the Athenian festival called the Adonia, women planted
so-called gardens of Adonis on housetops. Planted in shallow soil, these gardens
soon sprang up, and soon withered, thus symbolizing the early "death" of the
god.]

themselves and him who planted them, and are not unfruitful, but have in them seeds which may bear fruit in other natures, nurtured in other ways—making the seed everlasting and the possessors happy to the utmost extent of human happiness.

277

Phaedr. Yes, indeed, this is far nobler.

Soc. And now, Phaedrus, having agreed upon the premises we may decide about the conclusion.

Phaedr. About what conclusion?

Soc. About Lysias, whom we censured, and his art of writing, and his discourses, and the rhetorical skill or want of skill which was shown in them; for he brought up to this point. And I think that we are now pretty well informed about the nature of art and its opposite.

b

Phaedr. Yes, I think with you; but I wish that you would repeat what was said.

Soc. Until a man knows the truth of the several particulars of which he is writing or speaking, and is able to define them as they are, and having defined them again to divide them until they can be no longer divided, and until in like manner he is able to discern the nature of the soul and discover the different modes of discourse which are adapted to different natures, and to arrange and dispose them in such a way that the simple form of speech may be addressed to the simpler nature, and the complex and composite to the complex nature—until he has accomplished all this, he will be unable to handle arguments according to rules of art, as far as their nature allows them to be subjected to art, either for the purpose of teaching or persuading;—that is the view which is implied in the whole preceding argument.

c

Phaedr. Yes, that was our view, certainly.

Soc. Secondly, as to the justice of the censure which was passed on speaking or writing discourses—did not our previous argument show—?

d

Phaedr. Show what?

Soc. That whether Lysias or any other writer that ever was or will be, whether private man or statesman, writes a political treatise in his capacity of legislator, and fancies that there is a great certainty and clearness in his performance, the fact of his writing as he does is only a disgrace to him, whatever men

may say. For entire ignorance about the nature of justice and injustice, and good and evil, and the inability to distinguish the dream from the reality, cannot in truth be otherwise than dis-
e graceful to him, even though he have the applause of the whole world.

Phaedr. Certainly.

Soc. But he who thinks that in the written word there is necessarily much which is not serious, and that neither poetry nor prose, spoken or written, are of any great value—if, like the compositions of the rhapsodes,[1] they are only recited in order to be believed, and not with any view to criticism or instruc-
278 tion; and who thinks that even the best of them are but a reminiscence of what we know, and that only in principles of justice and goodness and nobility taught and communicated orally and written in the soul, which is the true way of writing, is there clearness and perfection and seriousness; and that such principles are like legitimate offspring;—being, in the first place, that which the man finds in his own bosom; secondly, the brethren and descendants and relations of this which has been duly
b implanted in the souls of others; and who cares for them and no others—this is the right sort of man; and you and I, Phaedrus, would pray that we may become like him.

Phaedr. That is most assuredly my desire and prayer.

Soc. And now the play is played out; and of rhetoric enough. Go and tell Lysias that to the fountain and school of the Nymphs
c we went down, and were bidden by them to convey a message to him and to other composers of speeches—to Homer and other writers of poems, whether set to music or not. And to Solon and the writers of political documents, which they term laws, we are to say that if their compositions are based on knowledge of the truth, and they can defend or prove them, when they are put to the test by spoken arguments, which leave their writings
d poor in comparison of them, then they are not only poets, orators, legislators, but worthy of a higher name.

Phaedr. What name is that?

Soc. Wise, I may not call them; for that is a great name

[1. Literally, "the stitchers of song" who recited the Homeric poems publicly at the Panathenaea, an Athenian festival celebrated every year]

which belongs to God only,—lovers of wisdom or philosophers in their modest [suitable] and befitting title.

Phaedr. Very good.

Soc. And he who cannot rise above his own compilations and compositions, which he has been long patching and piecing, adding some and taking away some, may be justly called poet or speechmaker or lawmaker.   e

Phaedr. Certainly.

Soc. Now go and tell this to your companion.

Phaedr. But there is also a friend of yours who ought not to be forgotten.

Soc. Who is that?

Phaedr. Isocrates the fair.[1]

Soc. What of him?

Phaedr. What message shall we send to him?

Soc. Isocrates is still young, Phaedrus; but I am willing to risk a prophecy concerning him.   279

Phaedr. What would you prophesy?

Soc. I think that he has a genius which soars above the orations of Lysias, and he has a character of a finer mold. My impression of him is that he will marvelously improve as he grows older, and that all former rhetoricians will be as children in comparison of him. And I believe that he will not be satisfied with this, but that some divine impulse will lead him to things higher still. For there is an element of philosophy in his nature. This   b is the message which comes from the gods dwelling in this place, and which I will myself deliver to Isocrates, who is my delight [darling] and do you give the order to Lysias who is yours.

Phaedr. I will; and now as the heat is abated let us depart.

Soc. Should we not offer up a prayer first of all to the local deities?

Phaedr. By all means.

Soc. Beloved Pan, and all ye other gods who haunt this place, give me beauty in the inward soul; and may the outward and inward man be at one. May I reckon the wise to be the   c

---

[1. Athenian orator and rhetorician (436 to 338 B.C.). Aside from his skill as a rhetorician, Isocrates is important for his views on education and his political theories.]

wealthy, and may I have such a quantity of gold as none but the temperate can carry. Anything more? That prayer, I think, is enough for me.

Phaedr. Ask the same for me, for friends should have all things in common.

Soc. Let us go.

Symposium

PERSONS OF THE DIALOGUE

APOLLODORUS, *who repeats*
to his companion the dia-
logue which he had heard
from Aristodemus, and
had already once narrated
to Glaucon.
PHAEDRUS.

PAUSANIAS.
ERYXIMACHUS.
ARISTOPHANES.
AGATHON.
SOCRATES.
ALCIBIADES. - *Promises to tell truth*
A TROOP OF REVELLERS.

SCENE:—The House of Agathon.

I believe that I am prepared with an answer. For the day be-   a
fore yesterday I was coming from my own home at Phalerum
to the city, and one of my acquaintance, who had caught a
sight of the back of me at a distance, in merry mood commanded me to halt: Apollodorus, he cried, O thou man of
Phalerum, halt! So I did as I was bid; and then he said, I was
looking for you, Apollodorus, only just now, that I might hear
about the discourses in praise of love, which were delivered by
Socrates, Alcibiades, and others at Agathon's supper. Phoenix,   b
the son of Philip, told another person who told me of them,
and he said that you knew; but he was himself very indistinct,
and I wish that you would give me an account of them. Who

but you should be the reporter of the words of your friend? And first tell me, he said, were you present at this meeting?

c Your informant, Glaucon, I said, must have been very indistinct indeed, if you can imagine that the occasion was recent, or that I could have been present.

Why, yes, he replied, that was my impression.

But how is that possible? I said. For Agathon has not been in Athens for many years, (are you aware of that?) and my acquaintance with Socrates, of whose every action and word I now make a daily study, is not as yet of three years' standing.

173 I used to be running about the world, thinking that I was doing something, and would have done anything rather than be a philosopher; I was almost as miserable as you are now.

Well, he said, cease from jesting, and tell me when the meeting occurred.

In our boyhood, I replied, when Agathon won the prize with his first tragedy, on the day after that on which he and his chorus offered the sacrifice of victory.

That is a long while ago, he said; and who told you—did Socrates?

b No indeed, I replied, but the same person who told Phoenix; —he was a little fellow, who never wore any shoes, Aristodemus, of the deme[1] of Cydathenaeum. He had been at this feast; and I think that there was no one in those days who was a more devoted admirer [lover] of Socrates. Moreover, I asked Socrates about the truth of some parts of his narrative, and he confirmed them. Then, said Glaucon, let us have the tale over again; is

c not the road to Athens made for conversation? And so we walked, and talked of the discourses on love; and therefore, as I said at first, I am prepared with an answer, and will have another rehearsal, if you like. For I love to speak or to hear others speak of philosophy; there is the greatest pleasure in that, to say nothing of the profit. But when I hear any other discourses, especially those of you rich men and traders, they are irksome to me; and I pity you who are my companions, because you always think

d that you are hard at work when really you are idling. And I dare say that you pity me in return, whom you regard as an

_____

[1. For "deme," see *Lysis* 205d]

unfortunate wight, which I perhaps am. But I certainly know of you what you only think of me—there is the difference.

Companion. I see, Apollodorus, that you are just the same —always speaking evil of yourself, and of others; and I do believe that you pity all mankind, beginning with yourself and including everybody else with the exception of Socrates, true in this to your old name, which, however deserved, I know not how you acquired, of Apollodorus the madman;[1] for your humor is always to be out of humor with yourself and with everybody except Socrates.

Apollodorus. Yes, friend, and I am proved to be mad, and out of my wits, because I have these notions of myself and you:[2] no other evidence is required.

Com. I have no wish to dispute about that, Apollodorus; but let me renew my request that you would repeat the tale of love.

Apoll. Well, the tale of love was on this wise:—But perhaps I had better begin at the beginning, and endeavor to repeat to you the words as Aristodemus gave them.

He said that he met Socrates fresh from the bath and sandalled; and as the sight of the sandals was unusual, he asked him whither he was going that he was so fine.

To a banquet at Agathon's, he replied, whom I refused yesterday, fearing the crowd that there would be at his sacrifice, but promising that I would come today instead; and I have put on my finery because he is a fine creature.[3] What say you to going with me unbidden?

Yes, I replied, I will go with you, if you like.

Follow then, he said, and let us demolish the proverb that

To the feasts of lesser men the good unbidden go;

instead of which our proverb will run that

e

174

b

[1. "Madman." The Greek reads *malakos,* which means, "soft, effeminate," or "fainthearted, yielding."]

[2. "Because I have these notions of myself and you." The Greek reads "because I am raging and (literally) striking a false blow or losing my wits concerning myself and you. *Parapaíō* ("to strike a false blow") may mean, in a more metaphorical sense, "to be infatuated."]

[3. Literally "I have prettified myself, so that I may go as a beautiful man (*kalos*) to a beautiful man's house."]

> To the feasts of the good unbidden go the good;

and this alteration may be supported by the authority of Homer, who not only demolishes but literally outrages this proverb. For, after picturing Agamemnon as the most valiant of men, he makes Menelaus, who is but a soft-hearted warrior, come of his own accord[1] to the sacrificial feast of Agamemnon, the worse to the better.

174c

I am afraid, Socrates, said Aristodemus, that I shall rather be the inferior person, who, like Menelaus in Homer,

> To the feasts of the wise unbidden goes.

d   But I shall say that I was bidden of you, and then you will have to make the excuse.

> Two going together,

he replied, in Homeric fashion, may invent an excuse by the way.[2]

This was the style of their conversation as they went along; and a comical thing happened—Socrates stayed behind in a fit of abstraction, and desired Aristodemus, who was waiting, to

e   go on before him. When he reached the house of Agathon he found the doors wide open, and a servant coming out met him, and led him at once into the banqueting-hall in which the guests were reclining, for the banquet was about to begin. Welcome, Aristodemus, said Agathon, you are just in time to sup with us; if you come on any other errand put that off, and make one of us, as I was looking for you yesterday and meant to have asked you, if I could have found you. But what have you done with Socrates?

I turned round and saw that Socrates was missing, and I had to explain that he had been with me a moment before, and that I came by his invitation.

You were quite right in coming, said Agathon; but where is he himself?

---

1. *Iliad,* xvii. 588.
2. *Iliad,* x. 224.

He was behind me just now, as I entered, he said, and   175
I cannot think what has become of him.

Go and look for him, boy, said Agathon, and bring him in;
do you, Aristodemus, meanwhile take the place by Eryximachus.

Then he said that the attendant assisted him to wash, and
that he lay down, and presently another servant came in and
said that our friend Socrates had retired into the portico of the
neighboring house. "There he is fixed, and when I call to him,"
said the servant, "he will not stir."

How strange, said Agathon; then you must call him again,
and keep calling him.

Let him alone, said my informant; he has just a habit of   b
stopping anywhere and losing himself without any reason; don't
disturb him, as I believe he will soon appear.

Well, if you say that, I will not interfere with him, said Agathon. My domestics, who on these occasions become my masters,
shall entertain us as their guests. "Put on the table whatever you
like," he said to the servants, "as usual when there is no one
to give you orders, which I never do. Imagine that you are our
hosts, and that I and the company are your guests; and treat
us well, and then we shall commend you." After this they supped;
and during the meal Agathon several times expressed a wish to   c
send for Socrates, but Aristodemus would not allow him; and
when the feast was half over—for the fit, as usual was not of
long duration—Socrates entered. Agathon, who was reclining
alone at the end of the table, begged that he would take the
place next to him; that I may touch the sage, he said and get
[enjoy, take advantage of] some of that wisdom which came into   d
your mind in the portion. For I am certain that you would not
have left until you had found what you were seeking.

How I wish, said Socrates, taking his place as he was desired,
that wisdom could be infused through the medium of touch,
out of the full into the empty man, like the water which the
wool sucks out of the full vessel into an empty one; in that
case how much I should prize sitting by you! For you would   e
have filled me full of gifts of wisdom, plenteous and fair, in
comparison of which my own is of a very mean and question-
able sort, no better than a dream; but yours is bright and only
beginning, and was manifested forth in all the splendor of youth

the day before yesterday in the presence of more than thirty thousand Hellenes.

You are insolent, said Agathon; and you and I will have to settle hereafter who bears off the palm of wisdom, and of this Dionysus shall be the judge; but at present you are better occupied with the banquet.

176   Socrates took his place on the couch; and when the meal was ended, and the libations offered, and after a hymn had been sung to the god, and there had been the usual ceremonies,— as they were about to commence drinking, Pausanias reminded them that they had had a bout yesterday, from which he and most of them were still suffering, and they ought to be allowed to recover, and not go on drinking today. He would therefore
b   ask, How the drinking could be made easiest?

I entirely agree, said Aristophanes, that we should, by all means, get off the drinking, having been myself one of those who were yesterday drowned in drink.

I think that you are right, said Eryximachus, the son of Acumenus; but I should like to hear one other person speak. What are the inclinations of our host?

I am not able to drink, said Agathon.

c   Then, said Eryximachus, the weak heads like myself, Aristodemus, Phaedrus, and others who never can drink, are fortunate in finding that the stronger ones are not in a drinking mood. (I do not include Socrates, who is an exceptional being, and able either to drink or to abstain.) Well, then, as the company seem indisposed to drink much, I may be forgiven for
d   saying, as a physician, that drinking is a bad practice, which I never, if I can help, follow, and certainly do not recommend to another, least of all to any one who still feels the effects of yesterday's carouse.

I always follow what you advise, and especially what you prescribe as a physician, rejoined Phaedrus the Myrrhinusian, and the rest of the company, if they are wise, will do the same.

e   All agreed that drinking was not to be the order of the day. Then, said Eryximachus, as you are all agreed that drinking is to be voluntary, and that there is to be no compulsion, I move, in the next place, that the flute-girl, who has just made her appearance, be told to go away; she may play to herself, or, if she has a mind, to the women who are within.[1] But on this day let us have conversation instead; and, if you will allow me, I will tell you what sort of conversation. This proposal having been accepted, Eryximachus proceeded as follows:—

177

I will begin, he said, after the manner of Melanippe in Euripides,

Not mine the word

which I am about to speak, but that of Phaedrus. For he is in the habit of complaining that, whereas other gods have poems and hymns made in their honor by the poets, who are so many, the great and glorious god, Love, has not a single panegyrist or encomiast. Many sophists also, as for example the excellent Prodicus, have descanted in prose on the virtues of Heracles and other heroes; and, what is still more extraordinary, I have met with a philosophical work in which the utility of salt has been made the theme of an eloquent discourse; and many other like things have had a like honor bestowed upon them. And only to think that there should have been an eager interest created about them, and yet that to this day, as Phaedrus well and truly says, no one has ever dared worthily to hymn Love's praises. This mighty deity has been neglected wholly! Now I want to offer Phaedrus a contribution to his feast; nor do I see how the present company can, at this moment, do anything better than honor the god Love. And if you agree to this, there will be no lack of conversation; for I mean to propose that each of us in turn shall make a discourse in honor of Love. Let us have the best which he can make; and Phaedrus, who is sitting first on the left hand, and is the father of the thought, shall begin.

b

c

d

No one will oppose that, Eryximachus, said Socrates; I certainly cannot refuse to speak on the only subject[2] of which I profess to have any knowledge, and Agathon and Pausanias will surely assent; and there can be no doubt of Aristophanes, who is always in the company of Dionysus and Aphrodite; nor will any one disagree of those whom I see around me. The proposal,

e

[1. I.e., within their female quarters. See Introduction.]
[2. I.e., the erotic.]

as I am aware, may seem hard upon us whose place is last; but that does not matter if we hear some good speeches first. Let Phaedrus begin the praise of Love, and good luck to him. All the company expressed their assent, and desired him to do as Socrates bade him.

178   Aristodemus did not recollect all that was said, nor do I recollect all that he related to me; but I will tell you what I thought most worthy of remembrance, and what the chief speakers said.

Phaedrus began by affirming that Love is a mighty god, and wonderful among gods and men, but especially wonderful in his birth. For that he is the eldest of the gods is an honor to him;

b   and a proof of this is, that of his parents there is no memorial; neither poet nor prose-writer has ever affirmed that he had any. As Hesiod says:—

> First Chaos came, and then broad-bosomed Earth,
> The everlasting seat of all that is,
> And Love.

In other words, after Chaos, the Earth and Love, these two came into being. Also Parmenides[1] sings of the generation of the gods:—

> First in the train of gods, he molded Love.

c   And Acusilaus[2] agrees with Hesiod. Thus numerous are the witnesses which acknowledge Love to be the eldest of the gods. And not only is he the eldest, he is also the source of the greatest benefits to us. For I know not any greater blessing to a young man beginning life than a virtuous lover, or to the lover than a beloved youth. For the principle which ought to be the guide of men who would nobly live—that principle, I say, neither kindred, nor honor, nor wealth nor any other motive is able to implant

d   as surely as love. Of what am I speaking? Of the sense of honor and dishonor, without which neither states nor individuals ever

---

[1. Parmenides of Elea, fl. ca. 450 B.C. He was the author of a didactic poem on nature.]

[2. Acusilaus of Argos, who lived "before the Persian Wars," compiled *Genealogies* translating and correcting Hesiod. For Hesiod, see *Lysis* 215c.]

do any good or great work. And I say that a lover who is detected in doing any dishonorable act, or submitting through cowardice when any dishonor is done to him by another, will be more pained at being detected by his beloved than at being seen by his father, or his companions, or any one else. And the beloved has the same feeling about his love, when he again is seen on any disgraceful occasion. And if there were only some way of contriving that a state or an army should be made up of lovers and their loves, they would be the very best governors of their own city, abstaining from all dishonor, and emulating one another in honor; and when fighting at one another's side, although a mere handful, they would overcome all men.[1] For what lover would not choose rather to be seen by all mankind than by his beloved, either when abandoning his post or throwing away his arms? He would be ready to die a thousand deaths rather than endure this. Or who would desert his beloved or fail him in the hour of danger? The veriest coward would become an inspired hero, equal to the bravest, at such a time;[2] Love would inspire him. That courage which, as Homer says, the god breathes into the soul of heroes, Love of himself infuses into the lover.

Love will make men dare to die for their beloved; and women as well as men. Of this, Alcestis, the daughter of Pelias, is a monument to all Hellas; for she was willing to lay down her life on behalf of her husband, when no one else would, although he had a father and mother; but the tenderness of her love so far exceeded theirs, that they seemed to be as strangers to their own son, having no concern with him; and so noble did this action of hers appear, not only to men but also to the gods, that among the many who have done virtuously she was one of the very few to whom the gods have granted the privilege of returning to earth, in admiration of her virtue; such exceeding honor is paid by them to the devotion and virtue of love. But Orpheus, the son of Oeagrus, because he appeared to them

---

1. We adduce here the historical illustration of the Theban "Sacred Band," composed exclusively of pairs of homosexual lovers (cf. Xenophon, *Symposium* 8.32).]

[2. The Greek reflects Plato's class bias: The base, or lowly born man (*kakos*) will be raised to the level of an aristocrat (*aristos*) by Love.]

to be a cowardly harper, who did not dare to die for love, like Alcestis, but contrived to go down alive to Hades, was sent back by them without effecting his purpose; to him they showed an apparition only of her[1] whom he sought, but herself they would not give up; moreover, they afterwards caused him to suffer death at the hands of women, as the punishment of his

e   intrusiveness. Far other was the reward of the true love of Achilles towards his lover Patroclus—his lover and not his love (the notion that Patroclus was the beloved one is a foolish error into which Aeschylus has fallen, for Achilles was surely the fairer of the two, fairer also than all the other heroes; and he was much younger, as Homer informs us, and he had no beard).[2]

[180b] And greatly as the gods honor the virtue of love, still the return of love on the part of the beloved to the lover is more admired and valued and rewarded by them, for the lover has a nature more divine and more worthy of worship. Now Achilles was quite aware, for he had been told by his mother, that he might avoid death and return home, and live to a good old age, if he abstained from slaying Hector. Nevertheless he gave his life to revenge his friend, and dared to die, not only on his behalf,

180   but after his death. Wherefore the gods honored him even above Alcestis, and sent him to the Islands of the Blest. These are my reasons for affirming that Love is the eldest and noblest and mightiest of the gods, and the chiefest author and giver of happiness and virtue, in life and after death.

c   This, or something like this, was the speech of Phaedrus; and some other speeches followed which Aristodemus did not remember; the next which he repeated was that of Pausanias, who observed that the proposal of Phaedrus was too indiscriminate, and that Love ought not to be praised in this unqualified manner. If there were only one Love, then what he said would be well enough; but since there are more Loves than one, he should have begun by determining which of them was to be the

d   theme of our praises. I will amend this defect, he said; and first of all I will tell you which Love is worthy of praise, and then

---

[1. I.e., Eurydice]
[2. Jowett has done some transposing of the Greek text as found in Burnet's edition.]

try to hymn the praiseworthy one in a manner worthy of the god. For we all know that Love is inseparable from Aphrodite, and if there were only one Aphrodite, there would be only one Love; but as there are two goddesses there must be two Loves. For am I not right in asserting that there are two goddesses? The elder one, having no mother, who is called (the heavenly Aphrodite)—she is the daughter of Uranus; the younger, who is the daughter of Zeus and Dione, whom we call common; and the other Love who is her fellow worker may and must also   e
have the name of common, as the other is called heavenly. All the gods ought to have praise given to them, but still I must discriminate the attributes of the two Loves. For actions vary according to the manner of their performance. Take for example, that which we are now doing, drinking, singing and talking—these actions are not in themselves either good or evil, but turn   181
out in this or that way according to the mode of performing them; and when well done they are good, and when wrongly done they are evil; and in like manner not every love, but only that which has a noble purpose, is noble and worthy of praise. But the Love who is the son of the common Aphrodite is essentially common, and has no discrimination, being such as the meaner   b
sort of men feel, and is apt to be of women as well as of youths, and is of the body rather than of the soul—the most foolish beings are the objects of this love which desires only to gain an end, but never thinks of accomplishing the end nobly, and therefore does good and evil quite indiscriminately. The goddess who is his mother is far younger, and she was born of the union   c
of the male and female, and partakes of both sexes. But the son of the heavenly Aphrodite is sprung from a mother in whose birth the female has no part, but she is from the male only; this is that love which is of youths only, and the goddess being older has nothing of wantonness. Those who are inspired by this love turn to the male, and delight in him who is the more valiant and intelligent nature; any one may recognize the pure enthusiasts in the very character of their attachments.[1] For they love not   d
boys, but intelligent beings whose reason is beginning to be de-

---

[1. Literally, "One might recognize in the very pederasty (= love of youths) itself those who have been utterly aroused by this desire."]

veloped, much about the time at which their beards begin to
grow. And in choosing them as their companions, they mean
to be faithful to them, and to pass their whole life with them,
and be with them, and not to take them in their inexperience,
and deceive them, and play the fool with them, or run away
from one to another of them. But the love of young boys should
e   be forbidden by law, because their future is uncertain; they may
turn out good or bad, either in body or soul, and the affection
which is devoted to them may be thrown away; in this the good
are a law to themselves, and the coarser sort of lovers ought
to be restrained by force, as we restrain or attempt to restrain
182   them from fixing their affections on women of free birth. For
the abuse of a thing brings discredit on the lawful use, and this
has led some to deny the lawfulness of love when they see the
impropriety and evil of attachments of this sort; for surely nothing
that is decorously and lawfully done can justly be censured. Now
in most cities the practice about love is determined by a simple
b   rule, and is easily intelligible. But here and in Lacedaemon there
is a perplexity,—in Elis and Boeotia, having no gifts of eloquence,
they are very straightforward; the universal sentiment is simply
in favor of these connections, and no one, whether young or
old, has anything to say to their discredit. The reason is, as I
suppose, that they are men of few words in those parts, and
therefore the lovers do not like the trouble of pleading their suit.
But in Ionia and other places, and generally in countries which
are subject to the barbarians, loves of youghts share the evil repute
of philosophy and gymnastics, because they are inimical to tyranny;
c   for the interests of rulers require that their subjects should be
poor in spirit, and that there should be no strong bond of friendship
or society among them, and love, above all other motives, is
likely to inspire this, as our Athenian tyrants learned by experience;
for the love of Aristogeiton and the constancy of Harmodius[1]

[1. Aristogeiton, known as the tyrannicide, and Harmodius, both of noble
descent, planned to kill the Athenian tyrant Hippias and his younger brother
Hipparchus in 514 B.C. The plot miscarried and only Hipparchus was killed.
Harmodius was murdered immediately by Hippias' guards, Aristogeiton was
later arrested and executed. The constancy of the two friends became famous
and, after the overthrow of the tyranny, they were celebrated in song and with
a statue set up in the public market.]

had a strength which undid their power. And, therefore, the ill
repute into which these attachments have fallen is to be ascribed   d
to the evil condition of those who make them to be ill-reputed;
that is to say, to the rapacity of the governors and the cowardice
of the governed; on the other hand, the indiscriminate honor
which is given to them in some countries is attributable to the
laziness of those who hold this opinion of them. There is yet
a more excellent way of legislating about them, which is our
own way; but this, as I was saying, is rather perplexing. For,
observe that open loves are held to be more honorable than secret
ones, and that the love of the noblest and highest, even if their
persons are less beautiful than others, is especially honorable.
Consider, too, how great is the encouragement which all the world
gives to the lover; neither is he supposed to be doing anything
dishonorable; but if he succeeds he is praised, and if he fail he
is blamed. And in the pursuit of his love the custom of mankind   e
allows him to do many strange things, which philosophy would
bitterly censure if they were done from any motive of interest,   183
or wish for office or power. He may pray, and entreat, and sup-
plicate, and swear, and be a servant of servants, and lie on a
mat at the door; in any other case friends and enemies would
be equally ready to prevent him, but now there is no friend who   b
will be ashamed of him and admonish him, and no enemy will
charge him with meanness or flattery; the actions of a lover have
a grace which ennobles them; and custom has decided that they
are highly commendable and that there is no loss of character
in them; and, what is yet more strange, he only may swear and
forswear himself (this is what the world says), and the gods will
forgive his transgression, for there is no such thing as a lover's
oath. Such is the entire liberty which gods and men allow
the lover, and which in our part of the world the custom confirms.   c
And this is one side of the question, which may make a man
fairly think that in this city to love and to be loved is held to
be a very honorable thing. But when there is a new regime, and
parents forbid their sons to talk with their lovers, and place them
under a tutor's care, and their companions and equals are personal
in their remarks when they see anything of this sort going on,
and their elders refuse to silence them and do not reprove their   d
words; anyone who reflects on this will, on the contrary, think

that we hold these practices to be disgraceful. But the truth, as I imagine, and as I said at first, is, that whether such practices are honorable or whether they are dishonorable is not a simple question; they are honorable to him who follows them honorably, dishonorable to him who follows them dishonorably. There is dishonor in yielding to the evil, or in an evil manner; but there is honor in yielding to the good, or in an honorable manner. Evil is the vulgar lover who loves the body rather than the soul,

e   and who is inconstant because he is a lover of the inconstant, and therefore when the bloom of youth which he was desiring is over, he takes wings and flies away, in spite of all his words and promises; whereas the love of the noble mind, which is in union with the unchangeable, is everlasting. The custom of our

184   country would have them both proven well and truly, and would have us yield to the one sort of love and avoid the other; testing them in contests and trials, which will show to which of the two classes the lover and the beloved respectively belong. And this is the reason why, in the first place, a hasty attachment is held to be dishonorable, because time is the true test of this as of most other things; and then again there is a dishonor in being overcome by the love of money, wealth, or of political power,

b   whether a man suffers and is frightened into surrender at the loss of them, or is unable to rise above the advantages of them. For none of these things are of a permanent or lasting nature; not to mention that no generous friendship ever sprang from them. There remains, then, only one way of honorable attachment which custom allows in the beloved, and this is the way of virtue; any service which the lover did was not to be accounted

c   flattery or dishonor, and the beloved has also one way of voluntary service which is not dishonorable, and this is virtuous service.

For we have a custom, and according to our custom any one who does service to another under the idea that he will be improved by him either in wisdom, or in some other particular of virtue—such a voluntary service as this, I say, is not regarded as a dishonor, and is not open to the charge of flattery. And these two customs, one the love of youth, and the other the

d   practice of philosophy and virtue in general, ought to meet in one, and then the beloved may honorably indulge the lover. For when the lover and beloved come together, having each of them

a law, and the lover on his part is ready to confer any favor
that he rightly can on his gracious loving one, and the other
is ready to yield any compliance that he rightly can to him who
is to make him wise and good; the one capable of communi-
cating wisdom and virtue, the other seeking after knowledge, and   e
making his object education and wisdom; when the two laws
of love are fulfilled and meet in one—then, and then only, may
the beloved yield with honor to the lover. Nor when love is of
this disinterested sort is there any disgrace in being deceived, but
in every other case there is equal disgrace in being or not being
deceived. For he who is gracious to his lover under the impres-   185
sion that he is rich, and is disappointed of his gains because
he turns out to be poor, is disgraced all the same: for he has
done his best to show that he would turn himself to anyone's
uses base for the sake of money, and this is not honorable. But
on the same principle he who lives for the sake of virtue, and
in the hope that he will be improved by his lover's company,
shows himself to be virtuous, even though the object of his affection be proved to be a villain, and to have no virtue; and
if he is deceived he has committed a noble error. For he has   b
proved that for his part he will do anything for anybody for
the sake of virtue and improvement, and nothing can be nobler
than this. Thus noble in every case is the acceptance of another
for the sake of virtue. This is that love which is the love of the
heavenly goddess, and is heavenly, and of great price to individuals and cities, making the lover and the beloved alike eager
in the work of their own improvement. But all other loves are
the offspring of the common or vulgar goddess. To you, Phaedrus,   c
I offer this my encomium of love, which is as good as I could
make on the sudden.

When Pausanias came to a pause (this is the balanced way
in which I have been taught by the wise to speak), Aristodemus
said that the turn of Aristophanes was next, but that either he
had eaten too much, or from some other cause he had the hiccough, and was obliged to change with Eryximachus the physician, who was reclining on the couch below him. Eryximachus,   d
he said, you ought either to stop my hiccough, or to speak in
my turn until I am better.

I will do both, said Eryximachus: I will speak in your turn,

and do you speak in mine; and while I am speaking let me recommend you to hold your breath, and if this fails, then to
e   gargle with a little water; and if the hiccough still continues, tickle your nose with something and sneeze; and if you sneeze once or twice, even the most violent hiccough is sure to go. In the meantime I will take your turn, and you shall take mine. I will do as you prescribe, said Aristophanes, and now get on.

Eryximachus spoke as follows: Seeing that Pausanias made a fair beginning, and but a lame ending. I will endeavor to sup-
186   ply his deficiency. I think that he has rightly distinguished two kinds of love. But my art instructs me that this double love is to be found in all animals and plants, and I may say in all that is; and is not merely an affection of the soul of man towards the fair, or towards anything; that, I say, is a view of the subject
b   which I seem to have gathered from my own art of medicine, which shows me how great and wonderful and universal is this deity, whose empire is over all that is, divine as well as human. And from medicine I will begin that I may do honor to my art. For there are in the human body two loves, which are confessedly different and unlike, and being unlike, have loves and desires which are unlike; and the desire of the healthy is one, and the desire of the diseased is another; and, as Pausanias says, the
c   good are to be accepted, and the bad are not to be accepted; and so too in the body the good and healthy elements are to be indulged, and the bad elements and the elements of desire are not to be indulged, but discouraged. And this is what the physician has to do, and in this the art of medicine consists: for medicine may be regarded generally as the knowledge of the loves and desires of the body, and how to fill or empty them; and the good physician is he who is able to separate fair love from
d   foul, or to convert one into the other; and if he is a skillful practitioner, he knows how to eradicate and how to implant love, whichever is required, and he can reconcile the most hostile elements in the constitution, and make them friends. Now the most hostile are the most opposite, such as hot and cold, moist and
e   dry, bitter and sweet, and the like. And my ancestor, Asclepius,[1] knowing how to implant friendship and accord in these elements,

---

[1. For Asclepius, see *Phaedrus* 270c.]

was the creator of our art, as our friends the poets here tell us, and I believe them; and not only medicine in every branch, but the arts of gymnastic and husbandry are under his dominion. Anyone who pays the least attention will also perceive that in music there is the same reconciliation of opposites; and I suppose that this must have been the meaning of Heracleitus, although his words are not accurate; for he says that one is united by disunion, like the harmony of the bow and the lyre. Now there is an absurdity in saying that harmony is disagreement or is composed of elements which are still in a state of disagreement. But perhaps what he really meant to say was that harmony is composed of differing notes of higher or lower pitch which disagreed once, but are now reconciled by the art of music; for if the higher and lower notes still disagree, there could be no harmony, as is indeed evident. For harmony is a symphony, and symphony is an agreement; but an agreement of disagreements while they disagree cannot exist; there is no harmony of discord and disagreement. This may be illustrated by rhythm, which is composed of elements short and long, once differing and now in accord; which accordance, as in the former instance, medicine, so in this, music implants, making love and unison to grow up among them: and thus music, too, is concerned with the principles of love in their application to harmony and rhythm. Again, in the abstract principles of harmony and rhythm there is no difficulty in discerning them, for as yet love has no double nature. But when you want to use them in actual life, either in the composition of music or in the correct performance of airs or meters composed already, which latter is called education, then the difficulty begins, and the good artist is needed. Then the old tale has to be repeated of fair and heavenly love—the love of Urania the fair and heavenly muse, and of the duty of accepting the temperate, and the intemperate only that they may become temperate, and of preserving their love; and again, of the vulgar Polyhymnia, who must be used with circumspection that the pleasure may not generate licentiousness; just as in my own art great skill is shown in gratifying the taste of the epicure without inflicting upon him the attendant evil of disease. The conclusion is that in music, in medicine, in all other things human as well as divine, both loves ought to be noted as far as may be, for they are both present.

187

b

c

d

e

188   The course of the season is also full of both principles; and
when, as I was saying, the elements of hot and cold, moist and
dry, attain the harmonious love of one another and blend in
temperance and harmony, they bring to men, animals, and vege-
tables health and wealth, and do them no harm; whereas the
wantonness and overbearingness of the other love affecting the
b   seasons is a great injurer and destroyer, and is the source of
pestilence, and brings many different sorts of diseases on animals
and plants; for hoar-frost and hail and blight spring from the
excesses and disorders of these elements of love, the knowledge
of which in relation to the revolutions of the heavenly bodies
and the seasons of the year is termed astronomy. Furthermore
all sacrifices and the whole art of divination, which is the art
c   of communion between gods and men—these, I say, are concerned only with the salvation and healing power of love. For
all impiety is likely to ensue if, instead of accepting and honoring
and reverencing the harmonious love in all his actions, a man
honors the other love, whether in his feelings towards gods or
parents, towards the living or the dead. Wherefore the business
of divination is to see to these loves and to heal them, and
divination is the peacemaker of gods and men, working by a
d   knowledge of the religious or irreligious tendencies which exist
in merely human loves. Such is the great and mighty, or rather
universal, force of all love. And that love, especially, which is
concerned with the good, and which is perfected in company
with temperance and justice, whether among gods or men, has
the greatest power, and is the source of all our happiness and
harmony and friendship with the gods which are above us, and
with one another. I dare say that I have omitted several things
e   which might be said in praise of Love, but this was not intentional,
and you, Aristophanes, may now supply the omission or take
some other line of commendation; as I perceive that you are
cured of the hiccough.

189   Yes, said Aristophanes, who followed, the hiccough is gone;
not, however, until I applied the sneezing; and I wonder whether
the principle of order in the human frame requires these sort
of noises and ticklings, for I no sooner applied the sneezing
than I was cured.

Eryximachus said: Take care, friend Aristophanes, you are

beginning with a joke, and I shall have to watch if you talk nonsense;   b
and the interruption will be occasioned by your own fault.

You are very right, said Aristophanes, laughing, and I will
retract what I said; and do you please not to watch me, as
I fear that in what I am going to say, instead of making others
laugh, which is to the manner born of our muse and would
be all the better, I shall only be laughed at by them.

Do you expect to shoot your bolt and escape Aristophanes?
Well, if you are very careful and have a due sense of respon-
sibility, I may be induced to let you off.   c

Aristophanes professed to open another vein of discourse;
he had a mind to praise Love in another way, not like that
either of Pausanias or Eryximachus. Mankind, he said, judging
by their neglect of him, have never, as I think, at all understood
the power of Love. For if they had understood him they would
surely have built noble temples and altars, and offered solemn
sacrifices in his honor; but this is not done, and certainly ought
to be done: for of all the gods he is the best friend of men,
the helper and the healer of the ills which are the great ob-   d
struction to the happiness of the race. I shall rehearse to you
his power, and you may repeat what I say to the rest of the
world. And first let me treat of the nature and state of man;
for the original human nature was not like the present, but
different. In the first place, the sexes were originally three in
number, not two as they are now; there was man, woman, and
the union of the two having a name corresponding to this dou-   e
ble nature;[1] this once had a real existence, but is now lost,
and the name only is preserved as a term of reproach. In the
second place, the primeval man was round and had four hands
and four feet, back and sides forming a circle, one head with
two faces, looking opposite ways, set on a round neck and
precisely alike; also four ears, two privy members, and the   190
remainder to correspond. When he had a mind he could walk
as men now do, and he could also roll over and over at a great
rate, leaning on his four hands and four feet, eight in all, like
tumblers going over and over with their legs in the air; this
was when he wanted to run fast. Now there were these three   b

---

[1. I.e., the androgynous]

sexes, because the sun, moon, and earth are three; and the man was originally the child of the sun, the woman of the earth, and the man-woman of the moon, which is made up of sun and earth, and they were all round and moved round and round like their parents. Terrible was their sight and strength, and the thoughts of their hearts were great, and they made an attack upon the gods; and of them is told the tale of Otus and Ephialtes who, as Homer says, dared to scale heaven, and would have laid hands upon the gods.[1] Doubt reigned in the councils of Zeus and of the gods. Should they kill them and annihilate the race with thunderbolts, as they had done the giants, then there would be an end of the sacrifice and worship which men offered to them; but, on the other hand, the gods could not suffer their insolence to be unrestrained. At last, after a good deal of reflection, Zeus discovered a way. He said: "I have a notion which will humble their pride and mend their manners; they shall continue to exist, but I will cut them in two and then they will be diminished in strength and increased in numbers; this will have the advantage of making them more profitable to us. They shall walk upright on two legs, and if they continue insolent and won't be quiet, I will split them again and they shall hop about on a single leg."[2] He spoke and cut them in two, like a sorb-apple which is halved for pickling, or as you might divide an egg with a hair; and as he cut them one after another, he bade Apollo give the face and the half of the neck a turn in order that the man might contemplate the section of himself: this would teach him a lesson of humility. He was also to heal their wounds and compose their forms. Apollo twisted the face and pulled the skin all round over that which in our language is called the belly, like the purses which draw in, and he made one mouth at the center, which he fastened in a knot (this is

190c

d

e

[1. Otus and Ephialtes were in Greek mythology the sons of Iphimedeia and the sea-god Poseidon. They grew, Homer tells us (*Odyssey* 11. 310–311), until they were "nine fathoms tall and nine cubits broad."]

[2. Specifically, "dancing as at the Askolia," the second day of the rural Dionysia, a rustic festival in honor of the wine-god Dionysus. Aristophanes, in his comedy *The Acharnians* (vv. 247ff.), describes one such festival, which featured the singing of lewd songs and the carrying of an enormous phallus in a procession.]

called the navel); he also molded the breast and took out most of the wrinkles, much as a shoemaker might smooth out leather upon a last; he left a few, however, in the region of the belly and navel, as a memorial of the primeval change. After the division the two parts of man, each desiring the other half, came together, and threw their arms about one another eager to grow into one, and would have perished from hunger without ever making an effort because they did not like to do anything apart; so when one of the halves died and the other survived, the survivor sought another mate, whether the section of an entire man or of an entire woman, which had usurped the name of man and woman, and clung to that. And this was being the destruction of them, when Zeus in pity invented a new plan: he turned the parts of generation round in front, for this was not always their position, and they sowed the seed no longer as hitherto like grasshoppers in the ground, but in one another; and after the transposition the male generated in the female in order that by the mutual embraces of man and woman they might breed, and the race might continue; or if man came to man they might be satisfied, and rest and go their ways to the business of life: so ancient is the desire of one another which is implanted in us, reuniting our original nature, making one of two, and healing the state of man. Each of us when separated is but the indenture of a man, having one side only like a flat fish, and he is always looking for his other half. Men who are a section of that double nature which was once called androgynous are lascivious;[1] adulterers are generally of this breed, and also adulterous and lascivious[2] women: the women who are a section of the woman don't care for men, but have female attachments; the female companions[3] are of this sort. But the men who are a section of the male follow the male, and while they are young, being a piece of the man, they hang about him and embrace him,[4]

b

c

d

e

[1. Literally, "fond of women" (*philogynaikes*)]

[2. Literally, "fond of men" (*philandroi*)]

[3. The Greek here is *hetaeristriae,* which literally means "female companions," but is used to denote lesbians.

[4. Rather, "They love men and delight in lying down beside and being entwined with men."]

and they are themselves the best of boys and youths, because
192   they have the most manly nature. Some indeed assert that they
are shameless, but this is not true; for they do not act thus
from any want of shame, but because they are valiant and manly, and have a manly countenance, and they embrace that which
is like them. And these when they grow up are our statesmen,
and these only, which is a great proof of the truth of what
I am saying. And when they reach manhood they are lovers
   b   of youth, and are not naturally inclined to marry or beget children, which they do, if at all, only in obedience to the law,
but they are satisfied if they may be allowed to live unwedded;
and such a nature is prone to love and ready to return love,[1]
always embracing that which is akin to him. And when one
of them finds his other half, whether he be a lover of youth
or a lover of another sort, the pair are lost in an amazement
   c   of love and friendship and intimacy, and one will not be out
of the other's sight, as I may say, even for a moment: these
are they who pass their lives with one another; yet they could
not explain what they desire of one another. For the intense
yearning which each of them has towards the other does not
appear to be the desire of intercourse, but of something else
which the soul desires and cannot tell, and of which she has
   d   only a dark and doubtful presentiment. Suppose Hephaestus,
with his instruments, to come to the pair who are lying side
by side and say to them, "What do you people want of one
another?" they would be unable to explain. And suppose further, that when he saw their perplexity he said: "Do you desire
to be wholly one; always day and night to be in one another's
company? For if this is what you desire, I am ready to melt
   e   you into one and let you grow together, so that being two you
shall become one, and while you live live a common life as
if you were a single man, and after your death in the world
below still be one departed soul instead of two—I ask whether
this is what you lovingly desire, and whether you are satisfied
to attain this?"—there is not a man among them when he heard
this who would deny or who would not acknowledge that this

[1. Rather, "Such a one is born a pederast (a lover of boys or youths)
and fond of having lovers."]

meeting and melting in one another's arms, this becoming one instead of two, was the very expression of his ancient need. And the reason is that human nature was originally one and we were a whole, and the desire and pursuit of the whole is called love. There was a time, I say, when the two were one, but now because of this wickedness of men God has dispersed us, as the Arcadians were dispersed into villages by the Lacedaemonians.[1] And if we are not obedient to the gods there is a danger that we shall be split up again and go about in basso-relievo, like the figures having only half a nose which are sculptured on columns, and that we shall be like tallies. Wherefore let us exhort all men to piety, that we may avoid the evil and obtain the good, of which Love is the lord and leader; and let no one oppose him—he is the enemy of the gods who opposes him. For if we are friends of God and reconciled to him we shall find our own true loves, which rarely happens in this world. I am serious, and therefore I must beg Eryximachus not to make fun or to find any allusion to Pausanias and Agathon,[2] who, as I believe, are of the manly sort such as I have been describing. But my words have a wider application—they include men and women everywhere; and I believe that if all of us obtained our love, and each one had his particular beloved, thus returning to his original nature, then our race would be happy. And if this would be best of all, that which would be best under present circumstances would be the nearest approach to such an union; and that will be the attainment of a congenial love. Therefore we shall do well to praise the god Love, who is the author of this gift, and who is also our greatest benefactor, leading us in this life back to our own nature, and giving us high hopes for the future, that if we are pious, he will restore us to our original state, and heal us and make us happy and blessed. This, Eryximachus, is my discourse of love, which, al-

193

b

c

d

[1. Arcadia, a mountainous region in the southern part of Greece, came under Spartan control in the mid-sixth century B.C. Being a land of small villages, Arcadia carried little weight in Greek politics.]

[2. The poetic strains of Agathon, considered voluptuous and effeminate by Aristophanes, were parodied in Aristophanes' comedy *Thesmophoriazusae,* or *The Ladies' Festival.*]

though different from yours, I must beg you to leave unassailed by the shafts of your ridicule, in order that each may have his e turn; each, or rather either, for Agathon and Socrates are the only ones left.

Indeed, I am not going to attack you, said Eryximachus, for I thought your speech charming, and did I not know that Agathon and Socrates are masters in the art of love, I should be really afraid that they would have nothing to say, after all the world of things which have been said already. But, for all that, I am not without hopes.

194 Socrates said: You did your part well, Eryximachus; but if you were as I am now, or rather as I shall be when Agathon has spoken, you would, indeed, be in a great strait.

You want to cast a spell over me, Socrates, said Agathon, in the hope that I may be disconcerted, thinking of the anticipation which the theater has of my fine speech.

I should be strangely forgetful, Agathon, replied Socrates, b of the courage and magnanimity which you showed when your own compositions were about to be exhibited, coming upon the stage with the actors and facing the whole theater altogether undismayed, if I thought that your nerves could be fluttered at a small party of friends.

Do you think, Socrates, said Agathon, that my head is so full of the theater as not to know how much more formidable to a man of sense a few good judges are than many fools?

c Nay, replied Socrates, I should be very wrong in attributing to you, Agathon, that or any other want of refinement. And I am quite aware that if you happened to meet with any one whom you thought wise, you would care for his opinion much more than for that of the many. But then we, having been a part of the foolish many in the theater, cannot be regarded as the select wise; though I know that if you chanced to light upon a really wise man, you would be ashamed of disgracing yourself before him—would you not?

Yes, said Agathon.

But you would not be ashamed of disgracing yourself before the many?

d Here Phaedrus interrupted them, saying: Don't answer him, my dear Agathon; for if he can only get a partner with whom he can talk, especially a good-looking one, he will no longer care about the completion of our plan. Now I love to hear him talk; but just at present I must not forget the encomium on Love which I ought to receive from him and every one. When you and he have paid the tribute to the god, then you may talk.

Very good, Phaedrus, said Agathon; I see no reason why   e
I should not proceed with my speech, as I shall have other opportunities of conversing with Socrates. Let me say first how I ought to speak, and then speak.

The previous speakers, instead of praising the god Love, or unfolding his nature, appear to have congratulated mankind on the benefits which he confers upon them. But I would rather praise the god first, and then speak of his gifts; this is always   195
the right way of praising everything. May I express unblamed then, that of all the blessed gods he is the blessedest and the best? And also the fairest, which I prove in this way: for, in the first place, Phaedrus, he is the youngest, and of his youth he is himself the witness, fleeing out of the way of age, which   b
is swift enough surely, swifter than most of us like: yet he cannot be overtaken by him; he is not a bird of that feather;[1] youth and love live and move together—like to like, as the proverb says. There are many things which Phaedrus said about Love in which I agree with him; but I cannot agree that he is older than Iapetus[2] and Kronos[3]—that is not the truth; as I maintain, he is the youngest of the gods, and youthful ever.   c
The ancient things of which Hesiod and parmenides speak, if they were done at all, were done of necessity and not of love; had love been in those days, there would have been no chaining or mutilation of the gods, or other violence, but peace and sweetness, as there is now in heaven, since the rule of Love began. Love is young and also tender; he ought to have a poet   d
like Homer to describe his tenderness, as Homer says of Ate, that she is a goddess and tender:—

[1. "He is not a bird of that feather." Rather, "Love's nature is to despise (old age) and not within a fair distance to approach him." Old age is being depicted as an old male lover whom Love, the beautiful boy, rejects.]

[2. In mythology, the son of Earth and Heaven]

[3. The youngest son of Earth and Heaven. Kronos castrated his father, Heaven.]

Her feet are tender, for she sets her steps,
Not on the ground but on the heads of men:

which is an excellent proof of her tenderness, because she walks
not upon the hard but upon the soft. Let us adduce a similar
proof of the tenderness of Love; for he walks not upon the
e   earth, not yet upon the skulls of men, which are hard, but in
[the softest of living things—] the hearts and souls of men: in
them he walks and dwells and has his home. Not in every soul
without exception, for where there is hardness he departs, where
there is softness there he dwells; and clinging always with his
feet and in all manner of ways in the softest of soft places,
196 how can he be other than the softest of all things? And he is
the youngest as well as the tenderest, and also he is of flexile
form; for without flexure he could not enfold all things, or wind
his way into and out of every soul of man without being discovered, if he were hard. And a proof of his flexibility and sym-
metry of form is his grace, which is universally admitted to be
in an expecial manner the attribute of Love; ungrace and love
are always at war with one another. The fairness of his com-
plexion is revealed by his habitation among the flowers; for he
b   dwells not amid unflowering or fading beauties, whether of body
or soul or aught else, but in the place of flowers and scents,
there he dwells and abides.

Enough of his beauty—of which, however, there is more
to tell. But I must now speak of his virtue: his greatest glory
is that he can neither do nor suffer wrong from any god or
any man; for he suffers not by force if he suffers, for force
c   comes not near him, neither does he act by force. For all serve
him of their own free will, and where there is love as well as
obedience, there, as the laws which are the lords of the city
say, is justice. And not only is he just but exceedingly temperate, for Temperance is the acknowledged ruler of the pleasures
and desires, and no pleasure ever masters Love; he is their mas-
d   ter and they are his servants; and if he conquers them he must
be temperate indeed. As to courage, even the God of War is
no match for him; he is the captive and Love is the lord, for
love, the love of Aphrodite, masters him, as the tale runs; and
the master is stronger than the servant. And if he conquers the

bravest of all he must be himself the bravest. Of his courage
and justice and temperance I have spoken; but I have yet to
speak of his wisdom, and I must try to do my best, according
to the measure of my ability. For in the first place he is a poet   e
(and here, like Eryximachus, I magnify my art), and he is also
the source of poesy in others, which he could not be if he were
not himself a poet. And at the touch of him every one becomes
a poet, even though he had no music in him before; this also
is a proof that Love is a good poet and accomplished in all
the musical arts; for no one can give to another that which
he has not himself, or teach that of which he has no knowledge.   197
Who will deny that the creation of the animals is his doing?
Are they not all the works of his wisdom, born and begotten
of him? And as to the artists, do we not know that he only
of them whom love inspires has the light of fame?—he whom
love touches not walks in darkness. The arts of medicine and
archery and divination were discovered by Apollo, under the
guidance of love and desire, so that he too is a disciple of love.
Also the melody of the Muses, the metallurgy of Hephaestus,   b
the weaving of Athene, the empire of Zeus over gods and men,
are all due to love, who was the inventor of them. Love set
in order the empire of the gods—the love of beauty, as is evident, for of deformity there is no love. And formerly, as I was
saying, dreadful deeds were done among the gods, because of
the rule of necessity; but now since the birth of love, and from
the love of the beautiful, has sprung every good in heaven and
earth. Therefore, Phaedrus, I say of love that he is the fairest   c
and best in himelf, and the cause of what is fairest and best
in all other things. And I have a mind to say of him in verse
that he is the god who

> Gives peace on earth and calms the stormy deep,
> Who stills the waves and bids the sufferer sleep.

He makes men to be of one mind at a banquet such as this,   d
fulfilling them with affection and emptying them of disaffection.
In sacrifices, banquets, dances, he is our lord—supplying kind-

ness and banishing unkindness, giving friendship and forgiving enmity, the joy of the good,[1] the wonder of the wise, the amazement of the gods; desired by those who have no part in him, and precious to those who have the better part in him; parent of delicacy, luxury, desire, fondness, softness,[2] grace; careful of the good, uncareful of the evil. In every word, work, wish,

e   fear—pilot, helper, defender, savior; glory of gods and men, leader best and brightest [most beautiful]: in whose footsteps let every [well-born] man follow, chanting a hymn and joining in that fair strain with which love charms the souls of gods and men. Such is the discourse, Phaedrus, half playful, yet having a certain measure of seriousness, which, according to my ability, I dedicate to the god.

198   When Agathon had done speaking, Aristodemus said that there was a general cheer; the fair youth was thought to have spoken in a manner worthy of himself, and of the god. And Socrates, looking at Eryximachus, said: Tell me, son of Acumenus, [did I just now seem to fear where no fear is, and] was I not a prophet? Did I not anticipate that Agathon would make a wonderful oration and that I should be in a strait?

I think, said Eryximachus, that you were right in the first anticipation, but not in the second.

b   Why, my dear friend, said Socrates, must not I or any one be in a strait who has to speak after such a rich and varied discourse as that? I am especially struck with the beauty of the concluding words—who could listen to them without amazement? When I reflected on the immeasurable inferiority of my own powers, I was ready to run away for shame, if there had been any escape. For I was reminded of Gorgias,[3] and at the end of his speech I fancied that Agathon was shaking at me the Gorginian or Gorgonian head of the great master of rhetoric, which was simply to turn me and my speech into stone, as Homer says, and strike me dumb. And then I perceived how foolish I had been in consenting to take my turn with you in

---

[1. Burnet follows the MSS reading "gently noble," or possibly "gentle-noble."]

[2. Or "effeminacy"]

[3. For Gorgias, see *Phaedrus* 261c.]

praising love, and saying that I too was a master of the art, when I really had no idea of the meaning of the word "praise," which appears to be another name for glorification, whether true or false; in which sense of the term I am unable to praise anything. For I in my simplicity imagined that the topics of praise should be true; this was to be the foundation, and that out of them the speaker was to choose the best and arrange them in the best order. And I felt quite proud, and thought that I could speak as well as another, as I knew the nature of true praise. Whereas I see now that the intention was to attribute to love every species of greatness and glory, whether   e
really belonging to him or not, without regard to truth or false- hood—that was no matter; for the original proposal seems to have been not that you should praise, but only that you should appear to praise him. And you attribute to love every imagin- able form of praise, and say that "he is all this," "the cause of all this," in order that you may exhibit him as the fairest   199
and best of all; and this of course imposes on the unwary, but not on those who know him: and a noble and solemn hymn of praise have you rehearsed. But as I misunderstood the na- ture of the praise when I said that I would take my turn, I must beg to be absolved from the promise which (as Euripides would say) was a promise of the lips and not of the mind. Fare- well then to such a strain: for that is not my way of praising; no, indeed, I cannot attain to that. But if you like to hear the truth about love, I am ready to speak in my own manner, though   b
I will not make myself ridiculous by entering into any rivalry with you. Say then, Phaedrus, whether you would like to have the truth about love, spoken in any words and in any order which may happen to come into my mind at the time. Will that be agreeable to you?

Aristodemus said that Phaedrus and the company bid him take his own course. Then, he said, let me have your permission first to ask Agathon a few more questions, in order that I may take his admissions as the premises of my discourse.

I grant the permission, said Phaedrus: put your questions.   c
Socrates then proceeded as follows:—

In the magnificent discourse, which you have uttered, I think that you were right, my dear Agathon, in saying that you would begin with the nature of love and then afterwards speak of his works—that is a way of beginning which I very much approve. And as you have spoken thus eloquently of the nature of love,

d   will you answer me a further question?—Is love the love of something or of nothing? And here I must explain myself: I do not want you to say that love is the love of a father or the love of a mother—that would be ridiculous; but to answer as you would, if I asked is a father a father of something? to which you would find no difficulty in replying, of a son or daughter: and that would be right.

Very true, said Agathon.

And you would say the same of a mother?

e   He assented.

Yet let me ask you one more question in order further to illustrate my meaning. Is not a brother to be regarded essentially as a brother of something?

Certainly, he replied.

That is, of a brother or sister?

Yes, he said.

And now, said Socrates, I will ask about love:— Is love of something or of nothing?

Of something, surely, he replied.

200   Keep in mind what this is, and tell me what I want to know—whether love desires that of which love is.

Yes, surely.

And does he possess, or does he not possess, that which he loves and desires?

Probably not, I should say.

Nay, replied Socrates, I would have you consider whether necessarily is not rather the word. The inference that he who desires something is in want of something, and that he who de-

b   sires nothing is in want of nothing, is in my judgment, Agathon, absolutely and necessarily true. What do you think?

I think with you, said Agathon, in that.

Very good. And would he who is great desire to be great, or he who is strong desire to be strong?

That would be inconsistent with our previous admissions.

True. For he who is anything cannot want to be that which he is?

Yery true.

But if, added Socrates, a man being strong desired to be strong, or being swift desired to be swift, or being healthy desired to be healthy (for anyone may be imagined to desire any quality which he already has), in these cases there might be an objection raised—they might be said to desire that which they have already. I give the example in order that we may avoid misconception. For as you may see, Agathon, these persons must be supposed to have their respective advantages at the time, whether they choose or not; and surely no man can desire that which he has. And therefore, when a person says, I am well and wish to be well, or I am rich and wish to be rich, and I desire simply what I have; we shall reply to him: "You, my friend, having wealth and health and strength, want to have the continuance of them; for at this moment, whether you choose or no, you have them. And when you say, I desire that which I have and nothing else, is not your meaning that you want to have what you now have in the future?" He must allow this?

c

d

He must, said Agathon.

Then, said Socrates, this is equivalent to desiring not what he has or possesses already, but that what he has may be preserved to him in the future?

Very true, he said.

e

Then he and everyone who desires, desires that which he has not already, and which is future and not present, and which he has not, and is not, and of which he is in want;—these are the sort of things which love and desire seek?

Yery true, he said.

Then now, said Socrates, let us recapitulate the argument. First, is not love of something, and of something too which is wanting to a man?

Yes, he replied.

201

Remember further what you said in your speech, or if you do not remember I will remind you: you said that the love of the beautiful disposes the empire of the gods, for that of deformed things there is no love—did you not say something like that?

Yes, said Agathon.

Yes, my friend, and the remark is a just one. And if this is true, love is the love of beauty and not of deformity?

He assented.

201b   And the admission has been already made that love is of that which a man wants and has not?

True, he said.

Then love wants and has not beauty?

Certainly, he replied.

And would you call that beautiful which wants and does not possess beauty?

Certainly not.

Then would you still say that love is beautiful?

Agathon replied: I fear that I did not understand what I was saying.

c   Nay, Agathon, replied Socrates [, you have spoken beautifully]; but I should like to ask you one more question:—Is not the good also the beautiful?

Yes.

Then in wanting the beautiful, love wants also the good?

I cannot refute you, Socrates, said Agathon. And let us suppose that what you say is true.

Say rather, dear Agathon, that you cannot refute the truth; for Socrates is easily refuted.

d   And now I will take my leave of you, and rehearse the tale of love which I heard once upon a time from Diotima of ~~God~~ HONOR Mantineia,[1] who was a wise woman in this and many other branches of knowledge. She was the same who deferred the plague of Athens[2] ten years by a sacrifice, and was my instructress in the art of love. In the attempt which I am about to make I shall pursue Agathon's method, and begin with his admissions, which are nearly if not quite the same which I made to the wise woman when she questioned me: this will be the easiest way, and I shall take both parts myself as well as I can. For, e   like Agathon, she spoke first of the being and nature of love, and then of his works. And I said to her in nearly the same

---

[1. Mantineia is located on south-east Arcadia, a mountainous area in the central Peloponnesus.]

[2. The Great Plague of Athens raged between 430–427 B.C. An account of the Plague is given in book 2 of Thucydides, *History of the Peloponnesian War*.]

HONOR UNCHANGEMB

words which he used to me, that love was a mighty god, and likewise fair; and she proved to me as I proved to him that, in my way of speaking about him, love was neither fair nor good. "What do you mean, Diotima," I said, "is love then evil and foul?" "Hush," she cried; "is that to be deemed foul which is not fair?" "Certainly," I said. "And is that which is not wise, ignorant? Do you not see that there is a mean between wisdom and ignorance?" "And what is this?" I said. "Right opinion," she replied, "which, as you know, being incapable of giving a reason, is not knowledge (for how could knowledge be devoid of reason? Nor again, ignorance, for neither can ignorance attain the truth), but is clearly something which is a mean between ignorance and wisdom." "Quite true," I replied. "Do not then insist," she said, "that what is not fair is of necessity foul, or what is not good evil; or infer that because love is not fair and good he is therefore foul and evil; for he is in a mean between them." "Well," I said, "love is surely admitted by all to be a great god." "By those who know or by those who don't know?" "By all." "And how, Socrates," she said with a smile, "can love be acknowledged to be a great god by those who say that he is not a god at all?" "And who are they?" I said. "You and I are two of them," she replied. "How can that be?" I said. "That is very intelligible," she replied; "as you yourself would acknowledge that the gods are happy and fair—of course you would—would you dare to say that any god was not?" "Certainly not," I replied. "And you mean by the happy, those who are the possessors of things good or fair?" "Yes." "And you admitted that love, because he was in want, desires those good and fair things of which he is in want?" "Yes, I admitted that." "But how can he be a god who has no share in the good or the fair?" "That is not to be supposed." "Then you see that you also deny the deity of love."

"What then is love?" I asked; "Is he mortal?" "No." "What then?" "As in the former instance, he is neither mortal nor immortal, but in a mean between them." "What is he then, Diotima?" "He is a great spirit (*daemon*), and like all that is spiritual he is intermediate between the divine and the mortal." "And what is the nature of this spiritual power?" I said. "This is the power," she said, "which interprets and conveys to the

202

b

c

d

e

LOVE COMPARED TO DISEASE

gods the prayers and sacrifices of men, and to men the commands
and rewards of the gods; and this power spans the chasm which
divides them, and in this all is bound together, and through
this the arts of the prophet and the priest, their sacrifices and
203   mysteries and charms, and all prophecy and incantation, find
their way. For God mingles not with man; and through this
power all the intercourse and speech of God with man, whether
awake or asleep, is carried on. The wisdom which understands
this is spiritual; all other wisdom, such as that of arts or handi-
crafts, is mean and vulgar. Now these spirits or intermediate
powers are many and divine [abundant], and one of them is
love." And who," I said, "was his father, and who his mother?"
b   "The tale," she said, "will take time; nevertheless I will tell you.
On the birthday of Aphrodite there was a feast of the gods,
at which the god Poros or Plenty, who is the son of Metis
or Discretion, was one of the guests. When the feast was over,
Penia or Poverty, as the manner was, came about the doors
to beg. Now Plenty, who was the worse for nectar (there was
no wine in those days), came into the garden of Zeus and fell
into a heavy sleep; and Poverty considering her own straitened
circumstances, plotted to have him for a husband,[1] and accord-
c   ingly she lay down at his side and conceived Love, who partly
because he is naturally a lover of the beautiful, and because
Aphrodite is herself beautiful, and also because he was born
on Aphrodite's birthday is her follower and attendant. And as
his parentage is, so also are his fortunes. In the first place he
is always poor, and anything but tender and fair, as the many
d   imagine him, and he is hard-featured and squalid, and has no
shoes nor a house to dwell in; on the bare earth exposed he
lies [without bedding] under the open heaven, in the streets,
or at the doors of houses, taking his rest; and like his mother
he is always in distress [he dwells with want]. Like his father
too, whom he also partly resembles, he is always plotting against
the fair and good; he is bold, enterprising, strong, a hunter of
men, always at some intrigue or other, keen in the pursuit of
wisdom, and never wanting resources; a philosopher at all times,
terrible as an enchanter, sorcerer, sophist; for as he is neither

Phil
because
he knows
_he is_
ignorant →
He is int
between
wisdom +
ignorance

[1. Rather, "she plotted to make for herself a child by Poros."]

mortal nor immortal, he is alive and flourishing at one moment when he is in plenty, and dead at another moment, and again alive by reason of his father's nature. But that which is always flowing in is always flowing out, and so he is never in want and never in wealth, and he is also in a mean between ignorance and knowledge. The truth of the matter is just this: No god is a philosopher or seeker after wisdom, for he is wise already; or does any one else who is wise seek after wisdom. Neither do the ignorant seek after wisdom. For herein is the evil of ignorance, that he who is neither good nor wise is nevertheless satisfied: he feels no want, and has therefore no desire."

204

"But who then, Diotima," I said, "are the lovers of wisdom, if they are neither the wise nor the foolish?" "A child may answer that question," she replied; "they are those who, like love, are in a mean between the two. For wisdom is a most beautiful thing, and love is of the beautiful; and therefore love is also a philosopher or lover of wisdom, and being a lover of wisdom is in a mean between the wise and the ignorant. And this again is a quality which Love inherits from his parents; for his father is wealthy and wise, and his mother poor and foolish. Such, my dear Socrates, is the nature of the spirit Love. The error in your conception of him was very natural, and as I imagine from what you say, has arisen out of a confusion of love and the beloved—this made you think that love was all beautiful. For the beloved is the truly beautiful, delicate, and perfect and blessed; but the principle of love is of another nature, and is such as I have described."

b

c

I said: "O thou stranger woman, thou sayest well, and now, assuming love to be such as you say, what is the use of him?" "That, Socrates," she replied, "I will proceed to unfold: of his nature and birth I have already spoken; and you acknowledge that love is of the beautiful. But someone will say: Of the beautiful in what, Socrates and Diotima—or rather let me put the question more clearly, and ask: When a man loves the beautiful, what does he love?" I answered her "That the beautiful may be his." "Still," she said, "The answer suggests a further question, which is this: What is given by the possession of beauty?" "That," I replied, "is a question to which I have no answer ready." "Then," she said, "let me put the word 'good' in the place of the beautiful,

d

e

and repeat the question: What does he who loves the good desire?" "The possession of the good," I said. "And what does he gain who possesses the good?" "Happiness," I replied; "there is no

205   difficulty in answering that." "Yes," she said, "the happy are made happy by the acquisition of good things. Nor is there any need to ask why a man desires happiness; the answer is already final." "That is true," I said. "And is this wish and this desire common to all? And do all men always desire their own good, or only some men?—what think you?" "All men," I replied; "the desire is common to all." "But all men, Socrates," she rejoined, "are not said to love, but only some of them; and you say that all

b   men are always loving the same things." "I myself wonder," I said, "why that is." "There is nothing to wonder at," she replied; "the reason is that one part of love is separated off and receives the name of the whole, but the other parts have other names." "Give an example," I said. She answered me as follows: "There is poetry, which, as you know, is complex and manifold. And all creation or passage of non-being into being is poetry or making,

c   and the processes of all art are creative; and the masters of arts are all poets." "Very true." "Still," she said, "you know that they are not called poets, but have other names; the generic term 'poetry' is confined to that specific art which is separated off from the rest of poetry, and is concerned with music and meter; and this is what is called poetry, and they who possess this kind of poetry

d   are called poets." "Very true," I said. "And the same holds of love. For you may say generally that all desire of good and happiness is due to the great and subtle power of love; but those who, having their affections set upon him, are yet diverted into the paths of money-making or gymnastic philosophy, are not called lovers—the name of the genus is reserved for those whose devotion takes one form only—they alone are said to love, or to be lovers." "In that," I said, "I am of opinion that you are

e   right." "Yes," she said, "and you hear people say that lovers are seeking for the half of themselves; but I say that they are seeking neither for the half, nor for the whole, unless the half or the whole be also a good. And they will cut off their own hands and feet and cast them away, if they are evil; for they love them not because they are their own, but because they are good, and dislike them not because they are another's but because they are evil. There is nothing which men love but the good. Do you think that there is?" "Indeed," I answered, "I should say not." "Then," she said, "the conclusion of the whole matter is, that men love the good." "Yes," I said. "To which may be added that they love the possession of the good?" "Yes, that may be added." "And not only the possession, but the everlasting possession of the good?" "That may be added too." "Then, love," she said, "may be described generally as the love of the everlasting possession of the good?" "That is most true," I said. | 206

"Then if this be the nature of love, can you tell me further," she said, "what is the manner of the pursuit? What are they doing who show all this eagerness and heat which is called love? Answer me that." "Nay, Diotima," I said, "if I had known I should not have wondered at your wisdom, or have come to you to learn." "Well," she said, "I will teach you;—love is only birth in beauty, whether of body or soul." "The oracle requires an explanation," I said; "I don't understand you." "I will make my meaning clearer," she replied. "I mean to say, that all men are bringing to the birth[1] in their bodies and in their souls. There is a certain age, at which human nature is desirous of procreation; and this procreation must be in beauty and not in deformity: and this is the mystery of man and woman,[2] which is a divine thing, for conception and generation are a principle of immortality in the mortal creature. And in the inharmonical they can never be. But the deformed is always inharmonical with the divine, and the beautiful harmonious. Beauty, then, is the destiny or goddess of parturition who presides at birth, and therefore when approaching beauty the conceiving power[3] is propitious, and diffuse, and benign,[4] and begets and bears fruit: on the appearance of foulness [it] frowns and contracts in pain, and is averted and morose, and shrinks up, and not without a pang refrains from conception. And this is the reason why, when the hour of conception arrives, and the teeming nature is full,[5] there is such a | b

c

d

[1. The Greek verb is *kyein,* which means "to conceive" or "to impregnate."]

[2. Rather, "The intercourse between man and woman is a parturition, or birth."]

[3. The Greek here is *to kyoun* (cf. *kyein* above): "the impregnating force."]

[4. Rather, "[The impregnating force] happily spreads out, or disperses."]

[5. "The teeming nature is full." Rather, "to the one who is impregnating and swelling with passion . . ."]

nervousness, excitedness

nervous agitation, state of overpowering emotion

e flutter and ecstasy about beauty whose approach is the allevia-
tion of pain. For love Socrates, is not, as you imagine, the love
of the beautiful only." "What then?" "The love of generation and
birth in beauty." "Yes," I said. "Yes, indeed," she replied. "But
why of birth?" I said. "Because to the mortal, birth is a sort of
eternity and immortality," she replied; "and as has been already
207 admitted, all men will necessarily desire immortality together with
good, if love is of the everlasting possession of the good."

And this she taught me at various times when she spoke
of love. And on another occasion she said to me, "What is the
reason, Socrates, of this love, and the attendant desire? See you
not how all animals, birds as well as beasts, in their desire of
b procreation, are in agony when they take the infection of love;—
this begins with the desire of union, to which is added the care
of offspring, on behalf of whom the weakest are ready to battle
against the strongest even to the uttermost, and to die for them,
and will let themselves be tormented with hunger or suffer anything in order to maintain their offspring. Man may be supposed
to do this from reason; but why should animals have these pas-
c sionate feelings? Can you tell me why?" Again I replied, that
I did not know. She said to me: "And do you expect ever to
become a master in the art of love, if you do not know this?"
"But that," I said, "Diotima, is the reason why I come to you,
because, as I have told you already, I am aware that I want
a teacher; and I wish that you would explain to me this and
the other mysteries of love." "Marvel not at this," she said, "if
you believe that love is of the immortal, as we have already
d admitted; for here again, and on the same principle too, the
mortal nature is seeking as far as is possible to be everlasting
and immortal: and this is only to be attained by generation,
because the new is always left in the place of the old. For even
in the same individual there is succession and not absolute unity:
a man is called the same; but yet in the short interval which
elapses between youth and age, and in which every animal is
said to have life and identity, he is undergoing a perpetual process
of loss and reparation—hair, flesh, bones, blood, and the whole
e body are always changing. And this is true not only of the body,
but also of the soul, whose habits, tempers, opinions, desires,
pleasures, pains, fears, never remain the same in any one of

us, but are always coming and going. And what is yet more surprising is, that this is also true of knowledge; and not only does knowledge in general come and go, so that in this respect we are never the same; but particular knowledge also experiences a like change. For what is implied in the word "recollection," but the departure of knowledge, which is ever being forgotten and is renewed and preserved by recollection, appearing to be the same although in reality new, according to that law of succession by which all mortal things are preserved, not by absolute sameness of existence, but by substitution, the old worn-out mortality leaving another new and similar one behind—unlike the immortal in this, which is always the same and not another? And in this way, Socrates, the mortal body, or mortal anything, partakes of immortality; but the immortal in another way. Marvel not then at the love which all men have of their offspring; for that universal love and interest is for the sake of immortality."

When I heard this, I was astonished, and said: "Is this really true, O thou wise Diotima?" And she answered with all the authority of a sophist: "Of that, Socrates, you may be assured;— think only of the ambition of men, and you will marvel at their senselessness, unless you consider how they are stirred by the love of an immortality of fame. They are ready to run risks greater far than they would have run for their children, and to spend money and undergo any amount of toil, and even to die for the sake of leaving behind them a name which shall be eternal. Do you imagine that Alcestis[1] would have died on behalf of Admetus, or Achilles after Patroclus, or your own Codrus[2] in order to preserve the kingdom for his sons, if they had not imagined that the memory of their virtues, which is still retained among us, would be immortal? Nay," she said, "for I am persuaded that all men do all things for the sake of the glorious fame of immortal virtue, and the better they are the more they desire this; for they are ravished with the desire of the immortal.

"Men whose bodies only are creative,[3] betake themselves

208

b

c

d

e

[1. The mythological heroine Alcestis, who volunteered to die in place of her husband Admetus, was celebrated in a play by Euripides.]

[2. An early king of Athens]

[3. The Greek reads literally "men who are pregnant (*enkymones*) as to their bodies."]

to women and beget children—this is the character of their love;
their offspring, as they hope, will preserve their memory and
give them the blessedness and immortality which they desire in
209   the future. But creative souls—for there are men who are more
creative [are more pregnant] in their souls than in their bodies—
conceive that which is proper for the soul to conceive or retain.
And what are these conceptions?—wisdom and virtue in general.
And such creators are all poets and other artists who may be
said to have invention. But the greatest and fairest sort of wisdom
by far is that which is concerned with the ordering of states
and families, and which is called temperance and justice. And
b   he who in youth has the seed of these implanted in him and
is himself inspired [is pregnant in his soul] when he comes to
maturity desires to beget and generate. And he wanders about
seeking beauty that he may beget offspring—for in deformity
he will beget nothing—and embraces the beautiful rather than
the deformed; and when he finds a fair and noble and well-
nurtured soul, and there is union of the two in one person,
he gladly embraces him, and to such an one he is full of fair
c   speech about virtue and the nature and pursuits of a good man;
and he tries to educate him; and at the touch and presence of
the beautiful he brings forth the beautiful which he conceived
long before, and the beautiful is ever present with him and in
his memory even when absent, and in company they[1] tend that
which he brings forth, and they are bound together by a far
nearer tie and have a closer friendship than those who beget
mortal children, for the children who are their common offpsring
d   are fairer and more immortal. Who, when he thinks of Homer
and Hesiod and other great poets, would not rather have their
children than any ordinary human ones? Who would not emulate
them in the creation of children such as theirs, which have
preserved their memory and given them everlasting glory? Or
who would not have such children as Lycurgus[2] left behind
to be the saviors, not only of Lacedaemon, but of Hellas, as
one may say! There is Solon,[3] too, who is the revered father

---

[1. The man and his male lover]

[2. For Lycurgus, see *Phaedrus* 258c.]

[3. For Solon, see *Phaedrus* 258c.]

of Athenian laws; and many others there are in many other places, both among Hellenes and barbarians. All of them have done many noble works, and have been the parents of virtue of every kind, and many temples have been raised in honor of their children, which were never raised in honor of the mortal children of anyone.

e

"These are the lesser mysteries of love, into which even you, Socrates, may enter; to the greater and more hidden ones[1] which are the crown of these, and to which, if you pursue them in a right spirit, they will lead, I know not whether you will be able to attain. But I will do my utmost to inform you, and do, you follow if you can. For he who would proceed rightly in this matter should begin in youth to turn to beautiful forms; and first, if his instructor guide him rightly, he should learn to love one such form only—out of that he should create fair thoughts; and soon he would himself perceive that the beauty of one form is truly related to the beauty of another; and then if beauty in general is his pursuit, how foolish would he be not to recognize that the beauty in every form is one and the same! And when he perceives this he will abate his violent love of the one, which he will despise and deem a small thing, and will become a lover of all beautiful forms; this will lead him on to consider that the beauty of the mind is more honorable than the beauty of the outward form. So that if a virtuous soul have but a little comeliness, he will be content to love and tend him, and will search out and bring to the birth thoughts which may improve the young, until his beloved is compelled to contemplate and see the beauty of institutions and laws, and understand that all is of one kindred, and that personal beauty is only a trifle; and after laws and institutions he will lead him on to the sciences, that he may see their beauty, being not like a servant in love with the beauty of one youth or man or institution, himself a slave mean and calculating, but looking at the abundance of beauty and drawing towards the sea of beauty, and creating and beholding many fair and noble thoughts and notions in boundless love of wisdom; until at length he grows

210

b

c

d

[1. The Greek here is *epoptika,* a reference to the *epopteia,* or the viewing of sacred objects, the highest grade of initiation into the Eleusinian Mysteries.]

and waxes strong, and at last the vision is revealed to him of a single science, which is the science of beauty everywhere.

e To this I will proceed; please to give me your very best attention.

"For he who has been instructed thus far in the things of love, and who has learned to see the beautiful in due order and succession, when he comes toward the end will suddenly perceive a nature of wondrous beauty—and this, Socrates is that final cause of all our former toils, which in the first place is ever-

211 lasting—not growing and decaying, or waxing and waning; in the next place not fair in one point of view and foul in another, or at one time or in one relation or at one place fair, at another time or in another relation or at another place foul, as if fair to some and foul to others, or in the likeness of a face or hands or any other part of the bodily frame, or in any form of speech or knowledge, nor existing in any other being; as for example,

b an animal, whether in earth or heaven, but beauty only, absolute, separate, simple, and everlasting, which without diminution and without increase, or any change, is imparted to the ever-growing and perishing beauties of all other things. He who under the influence of true love rising upward[1] from these begins to see that beauty, is not far from the end. And the true order of go-

c ing or being led by another to the things of love, is to use the beauties of earth as steps along which he mounts upwards for the sake of that other beauty, going from one to two, and from two to all fair forms, and from fair forms to fair actions, and from fair actions to fair notions, until from fair notions he arrives at the notion of absolute beauty, and at last knows what the

d essence of beauty is. This, my dear Socrates," said the stranger of Mantineia, "is that life above all others which man should live, in the contemplation of beauty absolute; a beauty which if you once beheld, you would see not to be after the measure of gold, and garments, and fair boys and youths, which when you now behold you are in fond amazement, and you and many a one are content to live seeing only and conversing with them without meat or drink, if that were possible—you only want to be with them and to look at them. But what if man had eyes

e to see the true beauty—the divine beauty, I mean, pure and clear

---

[1. Rather, "the one rising upward through true pederasty (*paiderastein*)"]

and unalloyed, not clogged with the pollutions of mortality, and all the colors and vanities of human life—thither looking, and holding converse with the true beauty divine and simple, and bringing into being and educating true creations of virtue and not idols only? Do you not see that in that communion only, beholding beauty with the eye of the mind, he will be enabled to bring forth, not images of beauty, but realities; for he has hold not of an image but of a reality, and bringing forth and educating true virtue to become the friend of God and be immortal, if mortal man may. Would that be an ignoble life?"

212

Such, Phaedrus—and I speak not only to you, but to all men—were the words of Diotima; and I am persuaded of their truth. And being persuaded of them, I try to persuade others, that in the attainment of this end human nature will not easily find a better helper than love. And therefore, also, I say that every man ought to honor him as I myself honor him, and walk in his ways, and exhort others to do the same, even as I praise the power and spirit of love according to the measure of my ability now and ever.

b

The words which I have spoken, you, Phaedrus, may call an encomium of love, or anything else which you please.

c

When Socrates had done speaking, the company applauded, and Aristophanes was beginning to say something in answer to the allusion which Socrates had made to his own speech, when suddenly there was a great knocking at the door of the house, as of revellers, and the sound of a flute-girl was heard. Agathon told the attendants to go and see who were the intruders. "If they are friends of ours," he said, "invite them in, but if not say that the drinking is over." A little while afterwards they heard the voice of Alcibiades resounding in the court; he was in a great state of intoxication, and kept roaring and shouting "Where is Agathon? Lead me to Agathon," and at length, supported by the flute-girl and some of his companions, he found his way to them. "Hail friends," he said, appearing at the door crowned with a massive garland of ivy and wall-flowers, and having his head flowing with ribands. "Will you have a very drunken man as a companion of your revels? Or shall I crown Agathon, as was my intention in coming, and go my way? For I was unable to come yesterday, and therefore I come today,

d

e

carrying on my head these ribands, that taking them from my own head, I may crown the head of this fairest and wisest of men, as I may be allowed to call him. Will you laugh at me because I am drunk! Yet I know very well that I am speaking the truth, although you may laugh. But first tell me whether I shall come in on the understanding that I am drunk. Will
213   you drink with me or not?"

The company were vociferous in begging that he would take his place among them, and Agathon specially invited him. Thereupon he was led in by the people who were with him; and as he was being led he took the crown and ribands from his head, intending to crown Agathon, and had them before his eyes; this prevented him from seeing Socrates, who made way for him,
b   and Alcibiades took the vacant place between Agathon and Socrates, and in taking the place he embraced Agathon and crowned him. Take off his sandals, said Agathon, and let him make a third on the same couch.

By all means; but who makes the third partner in our revels? said Alcibiades, turning round and starting up as he caught sight of Socrates. By Heracles, he said, what is this? here is Socrates always lying in wait for me, and always, as his way is, coming
c   out at all sorts of unsuspected places: and now, what have you to say for yourself, and why are you lying here, where I perceive that you have contrived to find a place, not by a professor or lover of jokes, like Aristophanes, but by the fairest of the company?

Socrates turned to Agathon and said: I must ask you to protect me, Agathon; for this passion of his has grown quite
d   a serious matter. Since I became his admirer[1] I have never been allowed to speak to any other fair one, or so much as to look at them. If I do he goes wild with envy and jealousy, and not only abuses me but can hardly keep his hands off me, and at this moment he may do me some harm. Please to see to this, and either reconcile me to him, or, if he attempts violence, protect me, as I am in bodily fear of his mad and passionate attempts.

There can never be reconciliation between you and me, said
e   Alcibiades; but for the present I will defer your chastisement.

[1. Rather, "since the time I fell in love with him"]

And I must beg you, Agathon, to give me back some of the ribands that I may crown the marvellous head of this universal despot—I would not have him complain of me for crowning you, and neglecting him, who in conversation is the conqueror of all mankind; and this not once only, as you were the day before yesterday, but always. Then taking some of the ribands, he crowned Socrates, and again reclined. When he had lain down again, he said: You seem, my friends, to be sober, which is a thing not to be endured; you must drink—for that was the agreement which I made with you—and I elect myself master of the feast until you are well drunk. Let us have a large goblet, Agathon, or rather, he said, addressing the attendant, bring me that wine-cooler. The wine-cooler was a vessel holding more than two quarts which caught his eye—this he filled and emptied, and bid the attendant fill it again for Socrates. Observe, my friends, said Alcibiades, that my ingenious device will have no effect on Socrates, for he can drink any quantity of wine and not be at all nearer being drunk. Socrates drank the cup which the attendant filled for him.

214

Eryximachus said: What is this, Alcibiades? Are we to have neither conversation nor singing over our cups; but simply to drink as if we were thirsty?

b

Alcibiades replied: Hail, worthy son of a most wise and worthy sire.

The same to you, said Eryximachus; but what shall we do?

That I leave to you, said Alcibiades.

The wise physician skilled our wounds to heal

shall prescribe and we will obey. What do you want?

Well, Eryximachus said: Before you appeared a resolution was agreed to by us that each one in turn should speak a discourse in praise of love, and as good a one as he could: this was passed round from left to right; and as all of us have spoken, and you have not spoken but have well drunken, you ought to speak, and then impose upon Socrates any task which you please, and he on his right hand neighbor, and so on.

c

That is good, Eryximachus, said Alcibiades; and yet the comparison of a drunken man's speech with those of sober men d   is hardly fair; and I should like to know, sweet friend, whether you really believe what Socrates was just now saying; for I can assure you that the very reverse is the fact, and that if I praise anyone but himself in his presence, whether god or man, he will hardly keep his hands off me.

For shame [hold your tongue], said Socrates.

By Poseidon, said Alcibiades, there is no use in your denying this, for no creature will I praise in your presence.

Well then take your own course, said Eryximachus, and if you like praise Socrates.

e   What do you think, Eryximachus? said Alcibiades; shall I attack him and inflict the punishment in your presence?

What are you about? said Socrates; are you going to raise a laugh at me? Is that the meaning of your praise?

I am going to speak the truth, if you will permit me.

I not only permit you but exhort you to speak the truth.

Then I will begin at once, said Alcibiades, and if I say anything that is not true, you may interrupt me if you will, and say that I speak falsely, though my intention is to speak the

215 truth. But you must not wonder if I speak any how as things come into my mind; for the fluent and orderly enumeration of all your wonderful qualities is not a task the accomplishment of which is easy to a man in my condition.

I shall praise Socrates in a figure which shall appear to him to be a caricature, and yet I do not mean to laugh at him, but only to speak the truth. I say then, that he is exactly like the masks of Silenus,[1] which may be seen sitting in the statuaries'

b   shops,[2] having pipes and flutes in their mouths; and they are made to open in the middle, and there are images of gods inside them. I say also that he is like Marsyas the satyr. You will not deny, Socrates, that your face is like that of a satyr. Aye, and there is a resemblance in other points too. For example, you are a bully,—that I am in a position to prove by the evidences of

---

[1. A satyr. Satyrs, half-man and half-goat, were normally depicted with beards and great, staring eyes. They were well-known for their lasciviousness.]

[2. Specifically, "in the shops of the carvers of Hermae." Hermae were slender, column-shaped male figures, usually bearded and with a prominent phallus. These statues stood before doorways.]

witnesses, if you will not confess. And are you not a flute-player? That you are, and a far more wonderful performer than Marsyas. For he indeed with instruments charmed the souls of men by the power of his breath, as the performers of his music do still: for the melodies of Olympus are derived from the teaching of Marsyas, and these, whether they are played by a great master or by a miserable flute-girl, have a power which no others have; they alone possess the soul and reveal the wants of those who have needs of gods and mysteries, because they are inspired. But you produce the same effect with the voice only, and do not require the flute; that is the difference between you and him. When we hear any other speaker, even a very good one, his words produce absolutely no effect upon us in comparison, whereas the very fragments of you and your words, even at second-hand, and however imperfectly repeated, amaze and possess the souls of every man, woman, and child who comes within hearing of them. And if I were not afraid that you would think me drunk, I would have sworn as well as spoken to the influence which they have always had and still have over me. For my heart leaps within me more than that of any Corybantian reveller,[1] and my eyes rain tears when I hear them. And I observe that many others are affected in the same way. I have heard Pericles and other great orators, but though I thought that they spoke well, I never had any similar feelings; my soul was not stirred by them, nor was I angry at the thought of my own slavish state. But this Marsyas has often brought me to such a pass, that I have felt as if I could hardly endure the life which I am leading (this, Socrates, you admit); and I am conscious that if I did not shut my ears against him, and fly from the voice of the siren, he would detain me until I grew old sitting at his feet.[2] For he makes me confess that I ought not to live as I do, neglecting the wants of my own soul, and busying myself with the concerns of the Athenians; therefore I hold my ears and tear myself away from him. And he is the only person who ever made me ashamed, which you

c

d

e

216

b

[1. I.e., one in the service of the Phrygian goddess Cybele]

[2. Jowett has done some transposing of the Greek here, as elsewhere, and omitted after "I am conscious" the line "that if I should willingly offer my ears, I would not hold up [against him] but suffer the same things [and] . . ."]

might think not to be in my nature, and there is no one else who does the same. For I know that I cannot answer him or say that I ought not to do as he bids, but when I leave his presence the love of popularity gets the better of me. And therefore I run away and fly from him, and when I see him I am ashamed of

c what I have confessed to him. And many a time I wish that he were dead, and yet I know that I should be much more sorry than glad, if he were to die: so that I am at my wit's end.[1]

And this is what I and many others have suffered from the flute-playing of this satyr. Yet hear me once more while I show you how exact the image is, and how marvelous his power. For

d I am sure that none of you know him; but I know him and will describe him, as I have begun. See you how fond he is of the fair? He is always with them and is always being smitten by them, and then again he knows nothing and is ignorant of all things— that is the appearance which he puts on. Is he not like a Silenus in this? Yes, surely: that is, his outer mask, which is the carved head of the Silenus; but when he is opened, what temperance there is, as I may say to you, O my companions in drink, residing within. Know you that beauty and wealth and honor, at which the many

e wonder, are of no account with him, and are utterly despised by him: he regards not at all the persons who are gifted with them; mankind are nothing to him; all his life is spent in mocking and flouting at them [while he feigns ignorance]. But when I opened him, and looked within at his serious purpose, I saw in him divine and golden images of such fascinating beauty that I was ready

217 to do in a moment whatever Socrates commanded: (they may have escaped the observation of others, but I saw them). Now I thought that he was seriously enamored of my beauty, and this appeared to be a grand opportunity of hearing him tell what he knew, for I had a wonderful opinion of the attractions of my youth. In the prosecution of this design, when I next went to him, I sent away

b the attendant who usually accompanied me[2] (I will confess the

---

[1. "So that I am at my wit's end." Literally, "so that I do not know what use I shall make of this man."]

[2. "When I next went to him . . ." Rather, "Not having been allowed before this to be alone with him [Socrates] without an attendant, I sent the attendant away." Tutors or other servants normally accompanied well-born Athenian youths so that their young charges would not be molested.]

whole truth, and beg you to listen; and if I speak falsely, do you, Socrates, expose the falsehood). Well, he and I were alone together, and I thought that when there was nobody with us, I should hear him speak the language of love as lovers do,[1] and I was delighted. Not a word; he conversed as usual, and spent the day with me and then went away. Afterwards I challenged him to the palaestra;[2] and he wrestled and closed with me several times alone; I fancied that I might succeed in this way. Not a bit; there was no use in that. Lastly, as I had failed hitherto, I thought that I must use stronger measures and attack him boldly, as I had begun, and not give him up until I saw how the matter stood. So I invited him to supper, just as if he were a fair youth, and I a designing lover. He was not easily persuaded to come; he did, however, after a while accept the invitation, and when he came the first time, he wanted to go away at once as soon as supper was over, and I had not the face to detain him. The second time, still in pursuance of my design, after we had supped, I went on conversing far into the night, and when he wanted to go away, I pretended that the hour was late and that he had better remain. So he lay down on the next couch to me, the same on which he had supped, and there was no one else in the apartment. All this may be told without shame to anyone. But what follows I could hardly tell you if I were sober. Yet as the proverb says, "In vino veritas," whether there is in boys or not;[3] and therefore I must speak. Nor, again, should I be justified in concealing the lofty actions of Socrates as I come to praise him. Moreover I have felt the pang;[4] and he who has suffered, as they say, is willing to tell his fellow sufferers only, as they alone will be likely to understand him, and will not be extreme in judging of the sayings or doings which have been wrung from his agony. For I have been bitten by the viper too; I have known in my soul, or in my heart, or in some other part, that worst of pangs, more violent

c

d

e

218

[1. Specifically, an older male lover to a boy]

[2. Where men wrestled and otherwise consorted naked together]

[3. The Latin aphorism "in wine truth" seems hardly at home in a fourth-century Athenian setting. Literally, the Greek says, "Wine is truth both without children and with them," an allusion to the Greek proverb "Wine and children speak the truth."]

[4. That is, of one who has been bitten by the viper]

in ingenuous youth than any serpent's tooth, the pang of philosophy, which will make a man say or do anything. And you whom
b   I see around me, your Phaedrus, your Agathon, your Eryximachus, your Pausanias, your Aristodemus, your Aristophanes, all of you, and I need not say Socrates himself, have all had experience of the same madness and passion of philosophy. Therefore listen and excuse my doings then and my sayings now. But let the attendants and other profane and unmannered persons close the doors of their cars.

When the lamp was put out and servants had gone away,
c   I thought that I must be plain with him and have no more ambiguity. So I gave him a shake, and I said: "Socrates, are you asleep?" "No," he said. "Do you know what I am meditating?" What is that?" he said. "I think," I replied, "that of all the lovers whom I have ever had you are the only one who is worthy of me, and you appear to be too modest to speak.[1] Now I feel that I should be a tool to refuse you this or any other favor, and therefore I come to lay at your feet all that
d   I have and all that my friends have, in the hope that you will assist me in the way of virtue, which I desire above all things, and in which I believe that you can help me better than anyone else. And I am certainly of opinion that I should have more reason to be ashamed of what wise men would say if I were to refuse a favor to such as you, than of what fools would say if I granted it." When he heard this, he said in his ironical manner: "Friend Alcibiades, you have indeed an elevated aim
e   if what you say is true, and if there really is in me any power by which you may become better; truly you must see in me some rare beauty of a kind infinitely higher than that which I see in you. And if, seeing this, you mean to share with me and to exchange beauty for beauty, you will have greatly the advantage of me; you will gain real beauty in return for apear
219 ance—gold in exchange for brass. But look again, sweet friend, and see whether you are not deceived in me. The mind begins to grow critical when the bodily eye fails, and you have not come to that yet." Hearing this, I said: "I have told you my purpose, which is quite serious, and do you consider what you

---

[1. Rather, "to court [me]"]

think best for you and me." "That is good," he said; "at some
other time then we will consider and act as seems best about   b
this and about other matters." When I heard this answer I fancied
that he was smitten, and that my arrows wounded him, and
so without waiting to hear more I got up, and throwing my
coat about him crept under his threadbare cloak, as the time
of year was winter, and there I lay during the whole night having
this wonderful monster in my arms. You won't deny this, Socrates.   c
And yet, notwithstanding all this, he was so superior to my
solicitations, so contemptuous and derisive and disdainful of my
beauty—which really, as I believe, had some attractions—hear,
of judges; for judges you shall be of the haughty virtue of
Socrates—that in the morning when I awoke (let all the gods
and goddesses be my witnesses) I arose as from the couch of
a father or an elder brother.   d

What do you suppose must have been my feelings after
this rejection at the thought of my own dishonor? And yet I
could not help wondering at his natural temperance and self-
restraint and courage. I never could have thought that I should
have met with a man like him in wisdom and endurance. Neither could I be angry with him or renounce his company, any
more than I could hope to win him. For I well knew that if   e
Ajax[1] could not be wounded by steel, much less he by money;
and I had failed in my only chance of captivating him. So I
wandered about and was at my wit's end; no one was ever more
hopelessly enslaved by another. All this, as I should explain,
happened before he and I went on the expedition to Potidaea;[2]
there we messed together, and I had the opportunity of ob-
serving his extraordinary power of sustaining fatigue and going   220
without food when our supplies were intercepted at any place,
as will happen with an army. In the faculty of endurance he
was superior not only to me but to everybody; there was no

[1. One of the legendary Greek heroes who fought at Troy. There is a
story that Ajax as a baby had been made invulnerable by being wrapped in
Hercules' lion skin, except at one point—his "Achilles heel"—where the skin
had not touched him.]

[2. A Corinthian colony which revolted from the Athenian empire in 432
B.C., and was reduced by Athens in 430]

one to be compared to him. Yet at a festival he was the only person who had any real power of enjoyment, and though not willing to drink, he could if compelled beat us all at that, and the most wonderful thing of all was that no human being had ever seen Socrates drunk; and that, if I am not mistaken, will soon be tested. His endurance of cold was also surprising. There

220b was a severe frost, for the winter in that region is really tremendous, and everybody else either remained indoors, or if they went out had on no end of clothing, and were well shod, and had their feet swathed in felt and fleeces: in the midst of this, Socrates, with his bare feet on the ice, and in his ordinary dress, marched better than any of the other soldiers who had their shoes on, and they looked daggers at him because he seemed to despise them.

c   I have told you one tale, and now I must tell you another, which is worth hearing, of the doings and sufferings of this enduring man while he was on the expedition. One morning he was thinking about something which he could not resolve; and he would not give up, but continued thinking from early dawn until noon—there he stood fixed in thought; and at noon attention was drawn to him, and the rumor ran through the wondering crowd that Socrates had been standing and thinking about something ever since the break of day. At last, in the evening after supper, some Ionians out of curiosity (I should explain that this was not in winter but in summer), brought

d   out their mats and slept in the open air that they might watch him and see whether he would stand all night. There he stood all night as well as all day and the following morning; and with the return of light he offered up a prayer to the sun, and went his way. I will also tell, if you please—and indeed I am bound to tell—of his courage in battle; for who but he saved my life? Now this was the engagement in which I received the prize of

e   valor: for I was wounded and he would not leave me, but he rescued me and my arms; and he ought to have received the prize of valor which the generals wanted to confer on me partly on account of my rank, and I told them so (this Socrates will not impeach or deny), but he was more eager than the generals that I and not he should have the prize. There was another occasion on which he was very noticeable; this was in the flight

of the army after the battle of Delium,[1] and I had a better   221
opportunity of seeing him than at Potidaea as I was myself
on horseback, and therefore comparatively out of danger. He
and Laches were retreating as the troops were in flight, and
I met them and told them not to be discouraged, and promised
to remain with them; and there you might see him, Aristophanes,   b
as you describe, just as he is in the streets of Athens, stalking
like a pelican,[2] and rolling his eyes, calmly contemplating enemies as well as friends, and making very intelligible to anybody,
even from a distance, that whoever attacks him will be likely
to meet with a stout resistance; and in this way he and his
companion escaped—for these are the sort of persons who are
never touched in war; they only pursue those who are running
away headlong. I particularly observed how superior he was   c
to Laches in presence of mind. Many are the wonders of Socrates
which I might narrate in his praise; most of his ways might
perhaps be paralleled in others, but the most astonishing thing
of all is his absolute unlikeness to any human being that is or
ever has been. You may imagine Brasidas[3] and others to have
been like Achilles; or you may imagine Nestor and Antenor
to have been like Pericles; and the same may be said of other   d
famous men, but of this strange being you will never be able
to find any likeness however remote, either among men who
now are or who ever have been, except that which I have already
suggested of Silenus and the satyrs; and this is an allegory not
only of himself, but also of his words. For, although I forgot
to mention this before, his words are ridiculous when you first   e
hear them; he clothes himself in language that is as the skin
of the wanton satyr—for his talk is of pack-asses and smiths
and cobblers and curriers, and he is always repeating the same
things in the same words, so that an ignorant man who did
not know him might feel disposed to laugh at him; but he who
pierces the mask and sees what is within will find that they   222

[1. Site of an Athenian defeat in the war against Sparta (see Thucydides, *History* 4.7)]

[2. Literally, "swaggering," "holding his head high"]

[3. A Spartan general who fought against Athens in the Peloponnesian War and was greatly admired for his bravery]

are the only words which have a meaning in them, and also the most divine, abounding in fair examples of virtue, and of the largest discourse, or rather extending to the whole duty of a good and honorable man.

This, friends, is my praise of Socrates. I have added my blame of him for his ill-treatment of me; and he has ill-treated

b not only me, but Charmides the son of Glaucon, and Euthydemus the son of Diocles, and many others in the same way— beginning as their lover he has ended by making them pay their addresses to him. Wherefore I say to you, Agathon, "Be not deceived by him; learn from me and take warning, and don't be a fool and learn by experience," as the proverb says.

c When Alcibiades had done speaking, there was a laugh at his plainness of speech, as he seemed to be still in love with Socrates. You are sober, Alcibiades, said Socrates, or you would never have gone about to hide the purpose of your satyr's praises, for all this long story is only an ingenious circumlocution, the point of which comes in by the way at the end; you want to

d get up a quarrel between me and Agathon, and your notion is that I ought to love you and nobody else, and that you and you only ought to love Agathon. But the plot of this Satyric or Silenic drama has been detected, and you must not allow him, Agathon, to set us at variance.

e I believe you are right, said Agathon, and I am disposed to think that his intention in placing himself between you and me was only to divide us; but he shall gain nothing by that move, as I will go and lie in the couch next to you.

Yes, yes, replied Socrates, by all means come here and lie on the couch below me.

Alas, said Alcibiades, how am I fooled by this man: he is determined to get the better of me at every turn. I do beseech you, allow Agathon to lie between us.

Impossible, said Socrates, as you praised me, and I ought to praise my neighbor on the right, he will be out of order in praising me again when he ought rather to be praised by me, and I must entreat you to consent to this, and not be jeal-

223 ous, for I have a great desire to praise the youth.

Ha! ha! cried Agathon, I will rise instantly, that I may be praised by Socrates.

The usual way, said Alcibiades, where Socrates is, no one else has any chance with the fair, and now how readily has he invented a specious reason for attracting Agathon to himself.

Agathon arose in order that he might take his place on the couch by Socrates, when suddenly a band of revellers entered, and spoiled the order of the banquet. Someone who was going out having left the door open, they had found their way in, and made themselves at home; great confusion ensued, and everyone was compelled to drink large quantities of wine. Aristodemus said that Eryximachus, Phaedrus, and others went away—he himself fell asleep, and as the nights were long took a good rest: he was awakened towards daybreak by a crowing of cocks, and when he awoke, the others were either asleep, or had gone away; there remained awake only Socrates, Aristophanes, and Agathon, who were drinking out of a large goblet which they passed round, and Socrates was discoursing to them. Aristodemus did not hear the beginning of the discourse, and he was only half awake, but the chief thing which he remembered, was Socrates insisting to the other two that the genius of comedy was the same as that of tragedy, and that the writer of tragedy ought to be a writer of comedy also. To this they were compelled to assent, being sleepy, and not quite understanding his meaning. And first of all Aristophanes dropped, and then, when the day was already dawning, Agathon. Socrates, when he had put them to sleep, rose to depart, Aristodemus, as his manner was, following him. At the Lyceum he took a bath and passed the day as usual; and when evening came he retired to rest at his own home.

ORDER FORM

GREAT BOOKS IN PHILOSOPHY PAPERBACK SERIES

ETHICS

Aristotle—*The Nicomachean Ethics*	$6.95
Jeremy Bentham—*The Principles of Morals and Legislation*	6.95
Immanuel Kant—*The Fundamental Principles of the*	
Metaphysic of Morals	3.95
John Stuart Mill—*Utilitarianism*	3.95
George Edward Moore—*Principia Ethica*	6.95
Friedrich Nietzsche—*Beyond Good and Evil*	6.95
Bertrand Russell—*On Ethics, Sex, and Marriage*	
(edited by Al Seckel)	16.95
Benedict de Spinoza—*Ethics* and *The Improvement of the*	
Understanding	7.95

SOCIAL AND POLITICAL PHILOSOPHY

Aristotle—*The Politics*	5.95
Edmund Burke—*Reflections on the Revolution in France*	5.95
John Dewey—*Freedom and Culture*	8.95
G.W.F. Hegel—*The Philosophy of History*	8.95
Thomas Hobbes—*The Leviathan*	5.95
Sidney Hook—*Paradoxes of Freedom*	7.95
John Locke—*Second Treatise on Civil Government*	3.95
Niccolo Machiavelli—*The Prince*	3.95
Karl Marx/Frederick Engels—*The Economic and Philosophic*	
Manuscripts of 1844 and *The Communist Manifesto*	4.95
John Stuart Mill—*On Liberty*	3.95
John Stuart Mill—*On Socialism*	5.95
John Stuart Mill—*The Subjection of Women*	3.95
Thomas Paine—*Rights of Man*	5.95
Plato—*The Republic*	6.95
Jean-Jacques Rousseau—*The Social Contract*	4.95
Mary Wollstonecraft—*A Vindication of the Rights of Women*	5.95

METAPHYSICS/EPISTEMOLOGY

George Berkeley—*Three Dialogues Between Hylas and Philonous*	4.95
René Descartes—*Discourse on Method* and *The Meditations*	5.95
David Hume—*An Enquiry Concerning Human Understanding*	4.95
William James—*Pragmatism*	5.95
Immanuel Kant—*Critique of Pure Reason*	7.95
Plato—*The Euthyphro, Apology, Crito, and Phaedo*	3.95
Plato on Homosexuality: Lysis, Phaedrus, and *Symposium*	4.95
Bertrand Russell—*The Problems of Philosophy*	6.95

PHILOSOPHY OF RELIGION

Ludwig Feuerbach—*The Essence of Christianity*	7.95
David Hume—*Dialogues Concerning Natural Religion*	4.95
John Locke—*A Letter Concerning Toleration*	3.95
Thomas Paine—*The Age of Reason*	11.95
Bertrand Russell—*On God and Religion* (edited by Al Seckel)	16.95
Sextus Empiricus—*Outlines of Pyrrhonism*	6.95

SPECIAL—For your library . . . the entire collection of 38 "Great Books in Philosophy" available at a savings of more than 15%. Only $215.00 (plus $7.50 postage and handling). Please indicate "Great Books— Complete Set" on your order form.

The books listed can be obtained from your book dealer or directly from Prometheus Books. Please indicate the appropriate books. Remittance must accompany all orders from individuals. Please include $2.50 postage and handling for the first book and $1.25 for each additional title (maximum $7.50. NYS residents please add applicable sales tax.) **Prices subject to change without notice.**

Send to _____
Please type or print clearly)

Address _____

City _____ State _____ Zip _____

Amount enclosed _____

Charge my ☐ **VISA** ☐ **MasterCard**

Account # ⬚⬚⬚⬚⬚⬚⬚⬚⬚⬚⬚⬚⬚⬚⬚⬚

Exp. Date _____/_____ Tel.# _____

Signature _____

Prometheus Books Editorial Offices
700 E. Amherst St., Buffalo, New York 14215

Distribution Facilities
59 John Glenn Drive, Amherst, New York 14228

Phone Orders call toll free: (800) 421-0351
FAX: (716) 691-0137
Please allow 3-6 weeks for delivery